Conscious
Afternoon
Teas

Conscious Afternoon Teas

A Girlfriend's Guide *to* Inner Peace

JYL AUXTER

EDITED BY JENNIFER BACON

BALBOA PRESS

A DIVISION OF HAY HOUSE

Balboa Press books may be ordered through booksellers or by contacting:

Balboa Press
A Division of Hay House
1663 Liberty Drive
Bloomington, IN 47403
www.balboapress.com
1 (877) 407-4847

Because of the dynamic nature of the Internet, any web addresses or
links contained in this book may have changed since publication and
may no longer be valid. The views expressed in this work are solely those
of the author and do not necessarily reflect the views of the publisher,
and the publisher hereby disclaims any responsibility for them.

The author of this book does not dispense medical advice or prescribe the use
of any technique as a form of treatment for physical, emotional, or medical
problems without the advice of a physician, either directly or indirectly. The
intent of the author is only to offer information of a general nature to help
you in your quest for emotional and spiritual well-being. In the event you use
any of the information in this book for yourself, which is your constitutional
right, the author and the publisher assume no responsibility for your actions.

Any people depicted in stock imagery provided by Thinkstock are models,
and such images are being used for illustrative purposes only.
Certain stock imagery © Thinkstock.

Print information available on the last page.

ISBN: 978-1-5043-3637-6 (sc)
ISBN: 978-1-5043-3639-0 (hc)
ISBN: 978-1-5043-3638-3 (e)

Balboa Press rev. date: 07/27/2015

To the fearless woman who has embraced the act of self-exploration, you have paved the way to greater inner peace.

Ong Namo Guru Dev Namo

TABLE OF CONTENTS

GIRLFRIEND GIFT

The Conscious Afternoon Teas book is a gift for my beloved (your friend's name)

_____

Presented (date & time) _____

You're a special girlfriend (because) _____

_____

_____

_____

Love (your name) _____

Congratulation! You're invited to a Conscious Afternoon Tea

Date _____   Time _____

Location _____

Hello my friends,

It's time once again to party with a purpose. I hope you enjoyed the *Conscious Dinner Parties* book and are ready for the second *Girlfriend's Guide* in this three-part series. *Conscious Afternoon Teas* prepares you for the next step on a spiritual path and will continue to define the sacred woman within. Nine tea parties filled with mystical facts and playful trivia are the foundations for creating a moment to learn and grow.

As you may remember from reading *Conscious Dinner Parties*, it is all about having fun and cooking up some mindfulness while you embark upon some important life themes. The *Conscious Afternoon Teas* book offers a similar inspiring program to be used at home. It is a tool for discovering greater joy, spiritual understanding and answers to some of life's tough questions like, "Why am I here, and how do I find inner peace in a world of chaos?" On the lighter side, if you are fond of desserts, the recipes for the conscious tea parties are healthy and low in calories.

Whether you are reading this book on your own or inviting girlfriends to share the experience, it is your time to enjoy some peace and calm. Breathe in deeply then exhale negative thoughts that may be blocking your bliss and clarity of mind. The *Conscious Afternoon Teas* will empower you to discover a spiritually solid place of inner tranquility just as the title says: *A Girlfriend's Guide to Inner Peace.*

Enjoy yourself, and gift this book on the right occasion to a deserving friend. It is liberating to be spiritually grounded and a positive influence out into the world.

Blessings & Gratitude,
Jyl Auxter

INTRODUCTION

A balanced, healthy woman clearly perceives her worth and spiritual wholeness. She has mastered the act of self-inquiry and self-discovery.

The Conscious Journey

I t's teatime. The perfect occasion to slow down and create a peaceful moment. It is a scheduled break in a hectic day to appreciate a cup of hot tea and a delicious, warm dessert. For some of us, it is retreating to a comfy space within our homes where we can finally put our feet up and relax. *Conscious Afternoon Teas* offer an ideal opportunity for some quality downtime. Most of us are long overdue for a pause to simply sit still and reflect upon our lives.

Vibrant, healthy and peaceful women do the work to awaken from an unconscious state. They create space in their busy schedules to stop long enough to contemplate important life issues. These women roll up their sleeves, dig deep into the subconscious mind and heal. They shift energies around difficult emotions. Prejudices are cleared, along with the pain from the past and fears for the future. These gals are able to live in the moment with gratitude and grace.

This book emphasizes the importance of carving out some precious "me time" to make a conscious connection between health (physical, emotional and mental) and spirituality. When we allow ourselves a chance to calm down and look within, it can add years to a more joyful, peaceful and healthier life.

Go a head and take this well-deserved break. Conscious teatimes are quite different from traditional tea parties. This is an opportunity to bring sacredness into everyday life. The holistic intention for this essay is to offer examples of nine powerful tea parties, which are perfect for calming the nerves, centering the mind and reflecting on important truths.

After many years of assisting women from multicultural and diverse religious backgrounds with yoga, meditation and spiritual healings, I have discovered that inner peace and good health are greatly interconnected. Both are powerfully influenced by our beliefs. Unaware of our tricky subconscious mind, we cling to old and sometimes unhealthy stories about our lives. These convictions seem to be deeply woven into our DNA and can remain entwined in our lives until we are forced to awaken. Spiritual awakening requires silence, introspection and self-acceptance.

Praise the women! *Conscious Afternoon Teas* is the second book of the Girlfriend's Guide series. Both books have been written to help women flourish and offer a fresh perspective on life. As mentioned in *Conscious Dinner Parties*, women play a key role in supporting a spiritual awakening on this planet, and it starts by stepping inward to awaken ourselves.

Life will take on greater spiritual meaning as we find our peace and become more consciously anchored. In the past, the definition of the word consciousness was understood as a complex process describing ones' cultural, familial, educational and experiential background. Currently, the planet is going through a major shift of energies to the next level of consciousness, called *pure awareness*. Pure awareness means undistracted consciousness. It is a state induced by a mystical trance: without limits, free of thoughts and emotions. It is a straight connection to the God force or source energy. Pure awareness and its implications are affecting women globally, and it is time to discover this concept by creating a tea party.

A spiritual revolution is occurring throughout the world. This could be the reason behind certain personal and massive upheavals. *Conscious Afternoon Teas* offers ways to clear the clutter from our minds and hearts. Balance is critical as we move into the future. As our minds release the negative chatter, our hearts are able to soften. Consciousness is the theme to be embraced if we are to assimilate this powerful new, *love* revolution.

Ladies, it is time to be responsible for our lives by celebrating a powerful intention to self-heal with an afternoon tea. It is up to us to take back our power and shine. It is critical that we know how to quickly find inner peace. Being consciously anchored in the world plays an important role as we move forward on our life's journey. We are all spiritual beings whether we acknowledge it or not, and we are fast becoming powerful teachers and leaders for the future.

PART I

The Inner Playground

Women around the globe are coming together in a much different way than ever before. We seek greater meaning out of life with deeper friendships as we bring the ancient, sacred wisdom of the past into the present. Women now seem to have a better understanding and appreciation for these prized relics.

Besides being the title of this book, Conscious Afternoon Teas are workshops I host throughout the country, where women can explore their metaphysical interests. It is an occasion to bond with like-minded girlfriends and heal. A conscious tea offers the chance to create an inner journey where concepts like stillness, chakras and intuition start to have a larger significance in day-to-day living. These parties help liberate females as they come together in a grander way for mutual understanding and support.

Sacred reality

Close your eyes and take a deep inhale breath. Exhale long and slow and notice how you feel. Simply closing your eyes and breathing can immediately transition you into a peaceful state. It will seem like all your worldly concerns just melt away with the first exhale. Make sure to sit straight with a tall spine and uncross your legs so the energy can easily flow.

Continue to breathe deeply with eyes closed. Take your gaze inward and up toward the middle of the forehead. With every inhale, pull energy up from the ground through your body

toward the heavens. With each exhale, send this blessed energy back down to mother earth. Feel your head, shoulders, hips, legs and feet gently fall into a relaxed state. Try to release all the tension in your body and just let go. After a few breaths, allow a violet light to greet you on your inhale, while the exhale turns to a golden white light. Let your body absorb each light and notice a deeper sense of peace and calm. The violet light detoxifies our bodies, while the white light heals.

With time, the violet and golden lights will be easy to manifest, while the breath gently supports the body as it settles into a natural, comfortable position. You will come to discover a magical inner playground instead of a darkness filled with endless mind chatter. A sweet calm begins to take over as you learn to still the mind and love the body. In this new inner world, time has no relevance. Soon, the outer world will be defined by this rich inner experience.

This is how it all starts. A conscious inner journey begins by having the courage to close your eyes and not be afraid of the unknown. Conscious Afternoon Teas bring girlfriends together to master this new skill. As a group, it is easier to find a strong, peaceful connection with the spirit world. This deep link opens a safe place where all our treasures lie. The group's energy will provide security until this process begins to make greater sense. Little by little, the group association becomes less needed. Mastering peace and calm on your own takes on an intuitive quality.

Keep in mind our individual inner worlds are all very different. It will not do any good to compare or compete. This is a solo journey. Many of the answers you personally seek shall be revealed as you close your eyes and follow the breath. Yes, it is that easy. It's as if there is a supernatural highway of information located directly above your head, and you now have immediate access to it just by closing your eyes. Synchronicity drives a new outer world experience, all because you took the time to honor an inner journey.

Here is an example of how an inner journey will affect your life. As you are sitting with your eyes closed, thoughts of your sister come to mind. Then out of nowhere you begin to see apples. Shortly after this experience is over and you are back in a fully awakened state, there is a knock on the door and there stands your sister with a big bag of beautiful, red organic apples. You, my friend, have now become a new member of the supernatural highway club. Everything you need to know will be easily manifested and life becomes magical.

Gradually, this inner journey may offer insights into other worlds and glimpses of the future. Mystical visions now take on a life of their own, as unbelievable things start to happen to ordinary women. Mental questions seem to get answered by a robust, unknown invisible response. Your sensitivity to these worlds around you will grow as your intuition matures. This is how the spirit world communicates as it guides you through a spiritual shift.

This transition into deeper levels of consciousness can take weeks, months, years or a whole lifetime to fully unfold. During the change, you can experience great joy, truth, beauty, aliveness, perfection and creativity. It can feel like you just stepped into Nirvana, and there is an urgency to experience it all.

At the same time, negative emotions may surface, accompanied by great physical or emotional pain. An illness might present itself to give you permission to take time to do some inner processing. When a shift in consciousness becomes too overwhelming, pray and communicate to the universe, higher self, spirit guides or angels that you need help. As you ground with exercise, food, yoga and your daily spiritual practice, the process should calm down.

Sometimes, there won't be mystical visions or great aha moments. However, you will begin to notice a much deeper relationship with the invisible God force. In the past, you might have avoided the opportunity to mention to others your love for the Divine. All of a sudden, there is an abundant amount of blessed energy bubbling up from inside and all you want to do is share this love. You only see the beauty in every living object, which is a signal that the inner changes have progressed.

The benefits of a spiritual journey are many. Tapping into your true nature, divine purpose, spiritual knowingness and intuition will become your most cherished gifts. The soul reveals healing powers just by closing your eyes as you step out of one world and into another. Old beliefs are challenged. A metaphysical state takes over and life seems to change for the better. A profound sensitivity guides you to choose differently, as you eagerly step into a sacred vortex where life has greater meaning.

Some of us will spend a lifetime asking others for advice on our health problems, career choices, family issues and spiritual purpose. We have forgotten that we have all the answers within ourselves. The time is now to create your own sacred reality and embrace an inner journey. As the mind quiets to honor stillness, you will quickly identify with a unique inner voice. The key is to know YOUR truth, not another person's truth for you, distorted through their filters. We are seeking purity on this conscious tea-drinking journey.

After a while, a peaceful existence develops into a priority. You seek healthy solutions to life's little glitches and celebrate peaceful moments in the company of great girlfriends. It becomes easy to surrender into *what is* happening in your life with great acceptance. Old wounds are released as your vibration shifts. It is time for celebration. You have fully embraced this solo journey where the spirit world continuously awaits you with open arms.

PART II

Party Preparations

TEA

Tea originated in China as early as the 3rd century B.C. during the Zhou Dynasty. It was a novel beverage consumed by a select few and was considered to be a very powerful medicine. The Chinese believed tea had healing properties vital to major organs in the body. Monks used tea during sacred rituals and as a way to stay awake during long meditations. The spiritual and medicinal use for tea would soon spread from China out into the rest of the world for all to enjoy.

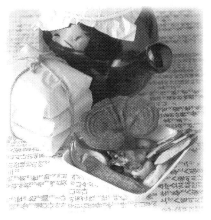

Your tea parties will bring ancient, spiritual wisdom and healing power into everyday life with an elaborate flair. While preparing for the afternoon parties, try to reflect on the legends of tea dating back centuries to monks and meditation. Connect with an inner monk-like persona. Reinforce the healing theme, and transform an area of your home into a monastery. It is time to bow your head in reverence, and humbly serve tea with an open heart to all of your favorite friends.

Before we start preparing for our parties, I would like to share one of my personal "Zen" moments with tea:

> I can still see the Buddhist monk, Thich Nhat Hanh as he walked into the meditation temple with his hands wrapped tightly around his modest cup of tea, as if it was a newly found treasure. The aroma and warmth captured

our attention and made it easier to lower the barriers around our guarded hearts and clouded minds.

As I slowly closed my eyes to begin meditation, I found myself longing for just one sip of the monk's infusion. I was sure his tea was the nectar of the Gods, and the secret to Samadhi (true Enlightenment). As I drifted into the calm of the neutral mind, I soon became consciously aware of my new mantra: tea, tea, tea...

Many healing benefits are posted under each tea profile. All infusions are considered to be a healthy afternoon choice. Most of the teas have caffeine. When serving a group, it is important to offer two pots of this heavenly beverage, one caffeine-free and one with caffeine. I have found that many women are very sensitive to the effects of caffeine and try to stay away from drinking it in the late afternoon. Also, the teas in this book are served hot, however during warm summer months, try to offer an iced version or a tea smoothie.

Essential oils are mentioned throughout the book. Pure, therapeutic, high-grade oils will play a major roll in our energy shifts and will support feeling good in our bodies. Each tea party offers an oil to be safely added into the teapots. Instructions on how many drops to use are provided. Have some fun as you play with essential oils. Let the oils shift the vibration of your afternoon cup of tea.

BAKING TIPS

L et's face it; the highlight of most girlie gatherings is the food on the menu. Afternoon teas would not be complete without a fabulous, healthy dessert to accompany an exceptional cup of imported tea. Baking is now on your to-do list. It is important to enjoy your guests on the day of the event. Try not to become overwhelmed with preparations or let them get in the way of enjoying your girlfriends. Consider shopping for ingredients well in advance. Do as much pre-planning as possible to ensure an idyllic atmosphere for your distinctive galas.

The recipes for each party are quite easy and require organic/Bio products. Local sustainable food is even better, and offers an opportunity to support your community's small organic farmers. This will ensure the very best food and tea for your gatherings. As a reminder, genetically modified foods (GMOs) are quickly making their way into the marketplace. In the USA and other countries around the world, these foods haven't been properly labeled as a possible danger to your health. Learn to be very conscious when choosing food, and make sure there are no GMOs on your buffet table. The saying is true, "We are what we eat." Conscious women consume only sustainable, healthy foods. Amen.

SWEET

W e often hear that refined sugars lack nutrients and if eaten in large quantities, they can cause an imbalance in the blood sugar affecting our metabolism. So, for many of us, a sugary dessert in the afternoon has become a big *No-No*. These conscious teas offer recipes for healthier snacks; ones you can count on to support the body. By using organic, natural ingredients to replace the old refined, white, beached sugar, you now have created a healthier dessert option. The list below offers alterative sweeteners with their health benefits and how to substitute them for white sugar in a recipe.

Raw Honey: Raw honey is a great choice for baking because it has not been processed, leaving more of the antioxidants, vitamins and minerals intact. When substituting honey for white sugar use ¾ cup honey for every 1 cup of sugar.

Powdered Honey: When a recipe calls for powdered sugar, try powdered honey instead for a healthier option. A cup of powdered honey can be substituted at a 1:1 ratio with powdered sugar.

Maple Syrup: Maple syrup is high in minerals like zinc and manganese. When baking with maple syrup, use ¾ cup syrup for 1 cup of granulated sugar.

Maple Crystals: When maple syrup is dehydrated it forms maple crystals. The substitution is a 1:1 ratio for white sugar. Maple crystals will add an additional soft fluffiness to your dessert.

Sucanat: Sucanat is dried sugar cane juice that has not been refined. It can be substituted at a 1:1 ratio for white sugar.

Agave Syrup: Agave syrup, sometimes referred to as Agave Nectar, consists primarily of fructose and glucose, with a lower glycemic level than white sugar. Substitute ½ cup of agave for 1 cup of sugar.

Dates: Date sugar is made of dehydrated ground dates and can be used as a 1:1 ratio substitute for white sugar. Dates are packed full of vitamins and are good for digestion.

Green Stevia: Stevia is significantly sweeter than white sugar; approximately 1 teaspoon can replace 1/4 cup of sugar. Green Stevia has a slight licorice flavor. It blends well when baking with citrus or chocolate flavors. For the best results, use Stevia in tandem with other sweeteners.

SAVVY

Conscious kitchens are very specific when it comes to the flour used in dessert recipes and follow the same guidelines as natural sweeteners. Use only organic flour that meets your health requirements. Refined white flour, like refined sugar, has very few natural vitamins and minerals. Flour plays a major role in most women's diets from breakfast bagels in the morning, to a sandwich at lunch and dinner rolls in the evening. Health practitioners have noticed that baking with certain flours may increase: depression, anxiety, fatigue, high blood pressure, heart attack, stroke, obesity and high cholesterol.

Wheat, oat, barley, spelt and rye flours all contain gluten, which is simply the protein that strengthens and binds dough in baking. Gluten has gotten such a bad reputation in the last couple of years, and maybe it is not the gluten itself that is so unhealthy and causing difficulty with digestion. The problem might be due to the unsustainable and contaminated grain in the marketplace today.

A friend shared recently that when she eats bread in the United States, she has all sorts of digestion issues. She actually gets quite sick. When she travels to her native country in the Middle East, she has no trouble with her digestion and enjoys eating wheat and other grains. Living in Europe now for seven years, I have noticed the quality of food, especially grain products, to be far superior to the products in the USA. This is very concerning.

An ancient grain being re-examined in the world today is called Einkorn. This grain has 65% lower levels of gluten, more vitamins and higher levels of proteins. Einkorn could serve as a healthier substitute for our contaminated wheat and high-glucose, gluten-free options. When so much emphasis is placed on processed gluten-free products, it upsets the natural balance of energy. Restoring balance now becomes critical. All of our gluten-free products in the market today may in the future prove to be not as supportive as we had hoped. Studies have already shown that people gain more weight from these products. The next problem arising from this gluten-free fad is higher than normal blood sugar levels. Try using Einkorn as a more balanced, healthy grain substitution.

When baking with gluten-free or wheat-free flours you may need to incorporate alternative binding agents. Recipes using flour substitutes have been carefully formulated to get the best possible result. However, exchanging flours can still be a risky experiment. So when using these new flour choices, it is important to be aware that there is no exact substitution. Changing the type of flour you use could result in a much different texture than a dessert made with standard pastry wheat flour and may require some adjustments like adding more liquid to the recipe. Below is a brief summary of some popular flours, their benefits and when to use them:

Einkorn Flour: Einkorn flour is the oldest and purest grain in the world today. Emmer is a hybrid of Einkorn and Spelt is a hybrid of Emmer. This flour has gluten, but about half as much as wheat, and it is higher in vitamins and proteins. 1 cup of Einkorn equals 1 ½ cup of flour.

Quinoa Flour: Quinoa flour contains plenty of healthy essential amino acids and can help to increase the alkalinity of the blood. It can be used for creating healthy cookies and cakes. Use quinoa in tandem with another flour. Quinoa flour is gluten-free.

Ground Soybeans: Soybean flour is high in calcium and fiber. It is known to have more than triple the protein of white pastry flour. This flour is gluten-free.

Almond Flour: Almond flour increases the alkalinity of the blood and is great to use with another flour for baking a healthy dessert. When almonds are sprouted the night before, the dessert will be more digestible with enhanced nutrients and preserved enzymes. Almond flour is gluten-free.

Hazelnut Flour: Ground hazelnuts boost the flavor of any baked goods. This flour works well for pie crusts. Use it with other flours, because it has a strong flavor. When making your own flour, simply grind hazelnuts into a fine texture. Rich in vitamin B and vitamin E, this nut flour is gluten-free.

Walnut Flour: Walnuts are great brain food and have many health benefits. This nut, when sprouted, is good to use in raw-food recipes. When grinding walnuts into flour, take care that it doesn't turn to butter; freeze the nuts before grinding. Walnut flour is gluten-free.

Barley Flour: Barley flour is high in fiber and does have gluten. This flour is said to lower blood cholesterol and sugar levels. Make sure to use the whole-grain variety when baking. Barley flour is best used to make biscuits, scones, breads and pancakes.

Flaxseed Flour: Flaxseed flour is gluten-free and rich in fiber, omega-3 fatty acids and essential nutrients like copper, magnesium, thiamine and manganese. Grind the flaxseeds into flour then add to your favorite dessert recipe.

Oat Flour: Oat flour does have gluten, but is a healthy substitution for wheat when baking. This flour goes rancid very quickly, so buy small amounts and store it in the fridge/freezer.

Buckwheat Flour: Buckwheat flour is not, despite its name, a form of wheat. Instead it is related to rhubarb. The small seeds of the plant are ground to make flour. It has a strong nutty taste, and is better to use with another flour when baking. Alternative names for this flour are: Beech Wheat, Kasha and Saracen Corn. This flour is gluten-free.

Chia Flour: Chia flour is made from ground chia seeds and is gluten-free. Highly nutritious, chia seeds have been labeled a super-food containing high levels of omega-3, fiber, calcium and protein. Sometimes called, "nature's healthy rocket fuel" this flour has been known to enhances energy levels.

In the end, the sugar and flour used to make your sanctified desserts are up to you. If substituting ingredients comes easily, then great. However, if this is your first time, enjoy the process and experiment with new textures and flavors. There are no mistakes when it comes to playing in the kitchen. If your dessert happens to come out of the oven not looking at all as you had hoped, scoop a spoonful into a bowl and serve it with a favorite homemade ice cream topped with a beautiful warm chocolate sauce. Who can say "no" to a dessert topped with ice cream and drizzled in warm cocoa?

There is one more conscious kitchen item to consider. Some of the recipes call for an essential oil to be used as an optional ingredient. Two drops of essential oils equals ¼ teaspoon of dried spices. It is truly fine not to include the oil, although you might be surprised how the flavor will be deeply enhanced, not to mention the shift in vibration that it adds to a simple dessert. As mentioned above, be sure to use only trusted, pure, therapeutic-grade essential oils in food. Never cook using oils diluted with unknown filler oils. Use these cheaper brands with a diffuser, as they create a wonderful calming ambiance during your tea party. Stay safe, and when you are not sure if your essential oil is a high quality one, don't use it in food.

Women, it is our duty to have conscious kitchens as we prepare for our tea parties. It is our responsibility to show our children how to create meals with healthy food. Many young sons and daughters today have never been taught to use food as a medicine for healing the body. Cook with the intention to nourish the body, mind and soul with energy from sustainable foods. As we open our hearts and prepare food for family members with varying dietary needs, we will learn what it truly means to love one another.

Bless all your tea party food just as you did for your dinner parties. A simple prayer or positive energy works well to change the vibration of the desserts. Trust your guests to notice. They will certainly applaud your efforts. Embrace becoming an alchemist in the kitchen and empower yourself to be a spiritual influence to the world.

Turn your home into an Ashram

Decorating tips

I t is time to transform an area of your home into a sanctuary, because it is good for your health. Let's name this space using the powerful ancient language of Sanskrit, and call your new sacred place Shanti (peace). The Buddhist and Hindu traditions say this word three times to represent peace of mind, body and speech. Your new sanctuary or *Shanti space* will be your special spot for creating inner harmony and grace.

No need to hire a special decorator or a feng shui expert. Don't get me wrong, interior designers and feng shui are very useful when creating a beautiful and highly functioning home. In this particular case, learn to trust your intuition. Empower yourself to bring forth everything needed to do the job in crafting a supportive space. Close your eyes, breathe and move into stillness. Ask Spirit to reveal the perfect place in your house to pray, meditate and serve tea. Also ask what components should be included in your Shanti space.

Get a pen and paper. Write down what has been revealed by the spirit world. Check your list against some of my favorite items: white candles, incense, a diffuser for essential oils, blankets, pillows, a couple of favorite essential oils and white sheepskins or soft floor rugs. Use nature to help create a balanced atmosphere in your home. Consider bringing the outside indoors with wild flowers, budded tree branches and fresh air from open windows. Also try adding the following natural elements to your Shanti space: earth, fire, water, air and spirit.

Each of the five elements will increase healthy energies by balancing the positive and negative ions in the environment. Fire creates action, while the Earth will ground and keep your life force in the present. Water is a clearing and cleansing element. Air will provide those aha mystical moments, angelic ideas and psychic gifts from the heavenly worlds. The energy from the elements makes it possible to call in the spirits. They exist among us all the time and, when consciously invited into our homes, they are guaranteed to heighten the energy in a jubilant way. All the elements protect you during those imperative growth moments.

Your Shanti space should always be clean and uncluttered. Sometimes it takes hosting a tea party to get organized and to find a place for all our belongings. I am a firm believer that a clear mind is an unencumbered home.

No matter what country I find myself living in, the first personal items to get unpacked and placed into my Shanti space are: an extra-long yoga mat, a Thai massage mattress, my sheepskins, crystals, a porcelain statue of Kuan Yin, a large tray of white candles and essential oils. It all goes in front of an extra large floor mirror. Ta Da…I present to you my peaceful home-zone, which never leaves that particular spot in the house until I am ready to pack up and move on. No matter what time of day, this is my favorite place to retreat.

So let's get started. Look around and decide where your peaceful area should be placed. The space ought to be away from doors, drafts or busy floor traffic. Contemplate whether you want to create an altar with photos, chimes, sage sticks, a water fountain and statues representing spiritual Deities. Do a little pre-planning, maybe some quick research on the Internet. See your Shanti space come together in your mind's eye. Before you know it, your new place of retreat is finished and ready to use.

A mirror can add a strong self-healing component. I know some of you might not like this idea. The ego, along with internal critical voices, might have a big problem seeing your reflection. It is important to embrace a loving response to the girl in the mirror. The seat of the soul and heart is found through the eyes, and studying them in the mirror will support your prayers, meditations, contemplations and movements.

Self-acceptance is extremely beneficial in a spiritual quest. The yogis believe every time we come to the yoga mat to practice, we start with a beginner's mind. Your reflection can create a fresh and humbling experience. It can be a useful aid as you become vulnerable to the healing process. As your vibration changes, so will your reflection.

Find your joy while decorating, and leave behind a personal signature. Customize your Shanti space on a budget using recycled objects. Let your self get carried away and think outside of the box. Try to be unique. Keep the space as open as possible. If you choose to ask others to join you, there ought to be enough room to accommodate extra girlfriends. I have personally learned if the place isn't pretty, soft, clean and cozy, I won't use it. Good luck creating your new haven. Show it off to friends and be pleased with yourself for being such a trendsetter.

PART III

Let the Parties Begin

Conscious Afternoon Teas

H ere are nine tea parties to promote healthy living. Prepare a dessert and tea, then sit down, relax and enjoy as you read one of the essays featured in the book. Every afternoon tea provides an organic dessert recipe, a recommended tea, a conscious contemplation and a teatime tune-up healing ritual. These tea parties are guaranteed to broaden the mind, balance the body and strengthen a spiritual connection. Please don't be afraid to embrace this opportunity.

Slow down and take time with this cathartic project. Have a pen ready to do some writing. Set clear intentions, and see where it leads. This may be a solo journey, one that is shared with girlfriends, or both. If you do plan to partake with others, make sure to have a diverse group of friends. Please plan on shifting some *mental marbles* as you create room in the mind to grow. Drop down from the head into the heart and feel some inspiring emotions. Surprise yourself with new results.

TEA PARTY I

Teatime Tip: *Close your eyes and breathe in the aroma of the tea. Have gratitude and feel a Divine presence.*

Sample Menu

Teacake Made from Fresh Organic Lemons
Enhanced with Essential Oil Infusion and
Topped with Raw Healing Honey

Matcha Genmaicha
(Japanese Healing Green Tea)
&
Lemongrass Tea

Conscious Contemplation
Finding Stillness

Teatime Tune-Ups
Mind, Body and Soul
Sacred Breathing

Recipe

Lemon Teacake

Ingredients

Cake

1 cup spelt flour
½ cup almond flour
¼ cup ghee (clarified butter)
¾ cup agave syrup
3 eggs, beaten
1 tablespoon fresh lemon juice
2 drops lemon essential oil
¾ teaspoon baking powder
Pinch sea salt

Lemon Glaze Frosting

½ cup water
3 medium lemons, juiced
4 drops lemon essential oil
4 drops tangarine essential oil
¼ cup raw honey

Preparation

Preheat oven to 350 degrees Fahrenheit. Grease one loaf pan and set aside.

In a mixing bowl, whisk together the ghee and agave. Fold in the eggs, lemon juice and essential oil. Gradually add flour and baking powder. Mix by hand or use an electric beater and blend until creamy then pour batter into a loaf pan. Bake for 35 minutes.

Meanwhile, prepare the frosting. Combine water, lemon juice, essential oils and honey in a small saucepan. Simmer and stir for 10 minutes. The glaze should thicken slightly, yet still be pourable.

Let the cake cool then place it on a serving tray. Pour the honey glaze over the top and allow it to run down the sides. Garnish with thinly sliced wheels of fresh lemons.

Tea

Matcha Genmaicha

Matcha is a tradition Japanese green tea that comes from the young leaves of the Camellia sinensis plant. It is steamed and stemmed before being ground into very fine green powder. This tea is known for its high-quality antioxidants and considered to be a miracle elixir. Matcha is a powerful super food that can also be used in baking favorite desserts.

Genmaicha is another Japanese tea known as brown rice tea. It was originally popular with lower class Japanese. Rice was used as filler making it an affordable tea. For this reason, the tea is called the *people's tea*. It is a popular choice for spiritual people who fast.

When the people's tea is combined with a high quality miracle elixir, expect a tasty and healthy tea. Your immune system will thank you. If you can't find this tea already combined, then buy each individually and mix yourself. I discovered this brilliant infusion while living in Belgium and it has become a favorite in the afternoon.

Optional essential oil: add a drop of Helichrysum to this infusion. This oil can serve as an excellent antioxidant.

Conscious Contemplation

Finding Stillness

Stilling the mind, emotions and body is a task that can seem to take forever, especially if you are in a hurry. This duty is not to be rushed. Every time you close your eyes to step into Divine stillness there is an opportunity to notice something more about yourself and the inner journey.

When embracing stillness, there are no expectations or rules. Set a kitchen timer for one minute to experience your first practice in stillness and then two minutes until you have built up to 10 minutes. With a little discipline, you will obtain great rewards of knowing authentic stillness without having to label it as meditation, enlightenment or Samadhi. Everyone knows what it means to be still; close your eye and breathe. From the time we were little children, we were told to keep still. As adult women, we are now creating positive vitality around this little word.

The first time I really appreciated what it truly meant to be still was when I was on a healing journey in Brazil. As I waited my turn in line to see the psychic surgeon, John of God, I was surprised to see so many people were slumped over in states of total inertness. Stillness in this case looked like everyone had left their bodies and was off to a wild party in the spirit world. If a pin dropped, you could have heard it. No one was moving but I will assure you, everyone was still breathing. This was a powerful image, which will stay lodged in my conscious mind for a long time.

Stillness allows the mind, body and soul a chance to recalibrate to a new vibration. For this reason, there tends to be an adjustment period. During moments of stillness, you are allowed to have thoughts and feelings. This offers an opportunity to observe the magnificence within. The purpose is to honor what you find and in some cases, release and heal it. Often our thoughts and emotions get in the way of perfect health. Stillness is the first teacher helping us to acknowledge an inner world. This new habit prepares us for great healing as we move into deeper core wounds later on in the journey.

For some, stillness may come easily, while others might find it to be a bit of a battle. On some days, your mind will be filled with chatter, while on other days stillness surrounds you. As you sit on the meditation cushion, you will start to know yourself better than you ever thought possible. Clarity of purpose is now available as you sit. Stillness can be soothing and blissful.

Yet at other times, this experience leads to edginess with great pain, fear, sadness and tremendous agitation. Old wounds and past lives may come to say, "Hello, I am still here." Embrace it all, because this adversity has come to help you grow. The trick is to learn how to go into the experience with an attitude of surrender, acceptance and grace.

Healing circles

Healing circles represent a powerful way to drink tea and bond with other women who are also new to the process of going within to discover an inner identity. It is a very spiritual event, especially when women come seeking health and healing. Conscious Afternoon Teas sometimes include a healing circle to support the inner shifts that must happen in order to establish a peaceful connection at a deeper level.

During these rituals, we learn to become sensitive to energy shifts and notice the powerful flow of spirit throughout our bodies. We don't break the circle to get up to go to the bathroom. This would be disrespectful to the other women. This is a serious connection and a powerful way to heal. Together as a group, a somewhat modified version of the *Ya, Ya Sisterhood*, we are united and become part of a greater oneness with the spirit world.

When your eyes close, a direct connection is established to the cosmos. Over time, this link helps you to become aware of a daily life force and purpose. Let's say the spirit realm provides a certain amount of energy to all of us each day to serve mankind. It is up to us to spend this energy wisely and to fulfill our dharma (purpose). If upon awakening, you start to think of something very upsetting, whew, there goes a huge amount of life force energy wasted.

This is called "leaking energy," and it just so happens that during moments of stillness, you will be able to identify where your life force energy is being lost. It is now up to you to change negative thinking patterns and create healthier boundaries. Time is required to heal dramas, traumas and mental abuse. Once under control, your energy will remain strong. You can now hold onto more life force and feel empowered throughout the day.

When healing old wounds from abuse and poor boundaries, you will need patience. As you move into stillness day after day, your awareness levels shift. You can now easily identify the healing work that must to be done. Identifying wounds is only one aspect of the self-healing process. Acceptance, surrender, forgiveness and unconditional love are next on the agenda. Don't rush. Healing can take a while and once the process starts, you may discover many emotional layers before discovering the core wound.

During stillness breaks, try to sit silently and notice everything that is happening around you; the clock is loudly ticking, birds are singing and the dishwasher has completed its cycle. See if you can keep bringing your attention back to the breath and an inner world. With time, stillness leads to deeper states of mindfulness and flows into seated meditations just like the example presented above when I was in Brazil. You too will look as if you have ditched your body for a wild party in the higher dimensions. For now, be okay with just working with stillness at least once a day and let the spirit world guide you on a magical journey of self-discovery.

What personal beliefs do you currently have about calming the mind and moving into stillness?

_____

_____

_____

_____

Has your spiritual awakening begun and if so, how do you know?

_____

_____

_____

_____

Is it physically uncomfortable to sit still? Describe.

_____

_____

_____

_____

Are you afraid to close your eyes and go within? Describe.

_____

_____

_____

_____

Teatime Tune-Ups

Get Still–– Inquire Actively––Live Consciously

Sit cross-legged, close your eyes and begin to rotate your torso in a large circle. Go in one direction for about 2 minutes, then do the same in the other direction. Feel the hips and knees open as sitting cross-legged becomes easier. Come back to the center and begin to connect with the breathing exercise below.

Sacred Breathing

Take deep inhales all the way below the navel center. On the inhale, feel the body expand. On the exhale, allow the navel to go inward toward the spine releasing the breath completely. With eyes closed, place your gaze at the brow point or "the third eye."

As you inhale (four counts), envision the breath coming from Mother Earth in through your feet and all the way up to the crown of your head. Hold the breath (four counts) and on the exhale (four counts), envision the breath leaving the top of your head and traveling back down your body to Mother Earth. Hold the breath out (four counts) and then continue.

Feel a big release at your hips on the exhale as you ground into Mother Earth. Stay with the sacred breath for at least 2-5 minutes.

Play with the rhythm of your breathing. You might find you can hold the breath for longer than four counts.

Health benefits

Conscious breathing can heal your body, strengthen your lungs and save your life by anchoring you in the present moment. When your focus is on the breath, the mind chatter quiets, making room for peace. If thoughts arise or you lose focus, simply return to the breath. The key to a peaceful life and a calm mind is sacred breathing.

Reflect once again on this concept of stillness. Notice if any other personal beliefs, fears or prejudices have now surfaced.

_____

_____

_____

_____

TEA PARTY II

Teatime Tip: *A Sweet dessert when served at a sacred tea party honors the sweetness in your life——simply enjoy.*

Sample Menu

Organic & Happy Watermelon Chia Cupcakes
Topped with Matcha Frosting

Japanese Jasmine Pearl Green Tea
&
Rooibos Jasmine Tea

Conscious Contemplation
Maintaining Good Health

Teatime Tune-Ups
Clearing the Path to a
New Vibration

Recipe

Watermelon Chia Cupcakes

Ingredients

Cupcake
1½ cups spelt flour
3 tablespoons chia seeds

2 teaspoons baking powder
Pinch sea salt
2 drops cinnamon essential oil
6 tablespoons ghee
2/3 cup maple syrup
2 eggs
½ cup plain yogurt
1 cup watermelon slices, juiced with pulp
1 slice beetroot, juiced

Matcha Frosting

½ cup goat cheese
¼ cup ghee
¾ cup powdered honey
2 tablespoons raw honey
1 tablespoon rice milk
1 teaspoon vanilla
2 teaspoons Matcha powder for coloring

Preparation

Preheat oven to 350 degree Fahrenheit. Grease one 12-cup muffin tin, or use paper liners. Set aside.

In a mixing bowl combine the ghee and maple syrup. Mix until creamy. Fold in the eggs, essential oil and yogurt. Set aside.

Juice the watermelon slices and beetroot together in a vegetable juicer. Add the juice to the liquid ingredients in the mixing bowl. The batter will change to a bright red color. Gradually add the dry ingredients and mix until batter is smooth. Fill cupcake tin or paper liners full. Bake for 20-25 minutes.

Meanwhile, prepare frosting. Blend goat cheese and ghee using a fork. Add powered honey and continue to blend. Fold in milk, vanilla and raw honey. For a light green color, add two teaspoons of Matcha powder and combine. Matcha will create a green color to resemble the rind of the watermelon and add an extra healthy feature. These muffins are very sweet, so dusting Matcha powder on top instead of frosting is an option.

Tea

Jasmine Pearl

Jasmine Pearls are hand-rolled bundles of green tea and jasmine flower. This delicious aromatic tea is found in Fujian, a province of China. When hot water is added, the pearls unfurl, releasing a tantalizing scent and amazing flavor.

Studies show Jasmine tea to be beneficial in treating depression and other illnesses. The medical benefits are mostly due to the antioxidants in green tea. As you inhale the sweet aroma from this tea, expect the nerves to calm, lungs to be supported and headaches released. Jasmine tea has also been reported by many to reduce cholesterol levels.

Optional essential oil: add a one of drop of Rose to this infusion. The aromatic influence is stimulating and elevating to the mind.

Conscious Contemplation

Maintaining good health

It just takes one health crisis in a woman's life to help define the meaning of balance and the importance of self-healing. Maintaining a sense of emotional, mental and spiritual balance is key, followed by nutrition, exercise, mindfulness and a spiritual practice. If you are able to heal yourself from an illness, mental disorder or acute pain, you will come to know that you and the spirit world are the ones responsible for healing your physical and subtle bodies. Doctors, energy healers, priests, psychologists and gurus can add support during difficult times, but you are the one doing the true healing work. Learn to trust the inner self-healing journey instead of being too quick to give your power away to an outside diagnosis.

Below are four easy steps to follow to maintain good health. Never lose hope while seeking self-healing. It may seem easier and faster to let someone else try to heal you, but in truth it will always come back to you. The sooner you embrace this life lesson the better it will be for your state of wellness.

4 Tips for maintaining a lifetime of good health

Tip #1 Nutrition

It is time to check in on your eating habits. Food is medicine. If you are a woman who lives on unsustainable, processed or GMO created foods, it is time to stop this dangerous eating habit and reconsider. We all know the importance of eating well. None of us will disagree. However, putting healthy eating into practice is a whole other story and can be very hard to do.

Bodies need a daily supply of minerals and vitamins that come from real food. It can be challenging to eat properly all the time. A key solution is to buy only organic/Bio foods that are good for the body and always have them on hand. Get into a new habit of putting a bag of raw organic almonds or carrots into your purse and carry them with you. When you are famished, grab a piece of fruit or a salad with loads of fresh seasonal vegetables. These foods will heal and nourish the body.

As you are preparing daily meals, try to have a plate of half raw items and half cooked foods. This will supply the combination of foods needed to help the body maintain proper digestion. Breakfast is an important meal. Lunch should be the biggest meal of the day. Dinner is light especially if you are trying to lose weight. Eliminate hard-to-digest animal proteins from dinner. Instead consume these proteins at breakfast and lunch.

What is a healthy diet for one person is not always a viable meal plan for another. Learn to honor your Ayurveda dosha and blood type. Eating for your dosha and blood type has gotten very popular over the last couple of decades. There are great books to read about both methods. Ayurvedic Medicine says that by understanding your body's constitution, or dosha, you can easily determine what foods will best support your body. If you are interested in discovering your personal dosha, there is a test in my book, *What's Cooking Within*. Many of my yoga students in the past have learned a great deal from taking this test and have applied it to living a healthier lifestyle.

What is your blood type? When I ask women, they seldom remember, but this can be important information for maintaining good health and eating properly. Are you O, A, AB⁻ (rare) or B? Certain blood types blend better with the protein lectins found in different foods. When you eat too many foods containing lectins incompatible with your blood type, it may cause health problems. This might affect digestion, insulin production, food metabolism and hormone balance. I had a student who always thought eating chicken was healthy because the media sold it as a better source of protein than red meat. When she found out her blood type was B, she immediately stopped eating chicken, lost 30 pounds and felt better than she had in a long time. According to the blood type diet, B types should stay clear of poultry.

The biggest single influence for determining your diet is listening to your body on a daily basis. If upon eating something, the stomach reacts with immediate pain, well, this is your body telling you to stop. What does your body think about becoming vegan? All your friends eat a vegan diet, and maybe you should too. It is time to ask yourself what is for your highest and best good. This calls for a new daily habit of muscle testing to take the mystery out of knowing what foods are best for your body.

What is muscle testing you ask? It is also known as Applied Kinesiology. The main premise is that your muscles will go weak when your body comes in contact with something it doesn't want or become strong with anything your body needs. You can have a naturopath show you or try it right now for yourself.

Stand with your feet hip distance apart and ask your body to show you, *yes or strong* and *no or weak*. For example, when I ask my body for yes or strong, I immediately fall forward. When I ask for no or weak, my body quickly moves backward. Once in awhile, a muscle test will neither be strong nor weak, in which case whatever food is being tested is considered neutral. Your body doesn't have a strong reaction either way.

Take an apple in your hand and place it on your chest. Ask your body if you should eat it or not. Your body will respond very quickly to the request. Then try the test with vitamins or a favorite alcoholic cocktail. For real fun, on small blank pieces of paper write down a number of different foods you consume on a daily basis and fold each paper in half so you can't see what has been written. Now pick up each piece of paper one-by-one and ask away. Let your body talk directly to you.

This is simply a reminder of all the healthy ways to stay empowered. The body changes everyday, and it is up to you to check in regularly to stay healthy. Ask your body if certain foods are GMO, or contain harmful pesticides or added hormones. With foods in the world being altered, it is very important to stay connected to the body. Check foods like wheat, nuts, soy products, corn or milk. These are often foods that cause problems to sensitive bodies. Soon when you reach for something to eat, you'll allow the body to immediately respond without thinking or doing anything. This is very helpful at the grocery store when considering new food items to try. Always muscle test first.

Try a new routine. Start the day off with what I like to call, *morning lifesavers*. The simply gesture of drinking warm water with lemon, honey and a splash of apple cider vinegar can really support the body in a profound way. Try drinking Green Magma or juice your own wheatgrass. Take a few of your favorite vegetables and juice them for your morning's breakfast. The body has been on an eight-hour food fast, so upon awaking, drink a beverage that can generate a healthy alkaline balance before sipping on coffee, drinking a favorite caffeinated tea or eating a sugary breakfast food.

When you embark upon a spiritual practice and tea parties, expect the diet to change significantly. You will crave healthier foods to support this important shift. Food becomes very important as you ground back into your body after an hour of a deep meditation practice. Never underestimate the power of a healthy balanced diet on a spiritual path.

Muscle test and ask the body if it is time for a detox. Try to remember to cleanse the body twice a year. The best times are in the spring and in the fall. Detox with vegetables, fruits and supportive herbs. Psyllium husk and hydrated bentonite clay can be used to support a deeper cleansing process. Be sure to drink plenty of water. During a detox, old emotions and physical pain may come up. You will soon start to feel better after the process has been completed.

It might be wise to consult an expert who can help you obtain maximum benefits. If you are battling with an illness, I recommend a proper cleanse that lasts 120 days. This is the amount of time it takes to clear the impurities from the blood. Yes, it takes 4 months to promote wellness. Most of us will cleanse for a week or two and that is usually a good amount of time.

Vegetable and fruit juices are always a big hit at an afternoon tea. In a juicing machine, combine spinach, kale, apple and carrot for an alkaline favorite. Try beetroot, celery and lemon to cleanse the body of toxins. Serve in a chilled goblet, and garnish with a fresh sprig of mint. Many women will be reminded how healthy and sustaining a freshly squeezed juice can be in the afternoon.

One final comment, if you start to feel a little sluggish, have your blood drawn to check for major health issues. I went to a Functioning Medicine professional who offered wonderful tips on my personal health, blood type and diet. The doctor made recommendations for a certain healing protocol that I hadn't considered, and it ended up being a valid resource.

Take a moment to move into stillness and connect to a deep place within. Ask yourself, if you are really eating the right foods for healing? Do you consider your food to be medicine for the body? Comment below.

_____

_____

_____

_____

It is time to muscle test yourself. Write about your experience.

_____

_____

_____

_____

Do you cleanse your body twice a year? If not make a plan.

_____

_____

_____

_____

Tip #2 Exercise

No one will say that exercise isn't important for staying healthy. However, research is now showing that over exercising can be dangerous for your health. We are seeking balance, so easy-does-it. Going to the gym isn't your only option these days, walking or going for a long bike ride in a peaceful place are other safe ways to move your energy. Turn up the music once in awhile, and dance a little. Stay in the body, feel your feet and move.

Learn to quickly get back into your body after medical emergencies. If you have been sick and are trying to get your health back, have faith. Rehabbing the body can be a challenge. You need to take it slow and have the courage to not give up. Stay away from making excuses. Keep reminding yourself that movement is a sacred act. Move into the pain with grace while you allow some time for your energy to purify and for the body to fully recover. Send love and acceptance to the pain and be prepared to see an immediate shift.

Once again, understanding your Ayurveda dosha, or mind-body constitution can aid in choosing the right exercise. Thin, small bone structured women should try walking, swimming, dancing, tennis and horseback riding. Maybe you are a more muscular, sporty type. Then running, jumping and competing in sports are better suited to you. However a tall, large boned woman has the opportunity to excel at intense power sports like basketball, triathlons, bodybuilding and soccer. Get a coach and see where your talent lies.

Moving your energy is good for the mind, body and soul and provides many positive results. If you don't have an exercise program, sit down right now and work out a plan by doing something you love. Riding a stationary bike is great fun while watching the food channel. Don't make it hard, or you won't do it.

As a side note, each of the teatime tune-ups is considered to be a form of movement that is extremely powerful for supporting good health. Please make sure to take the time to try all of them.

Are you getting enough exercise? If not make a plan.

_____

_____

_____

_____

What exercise compliments your body type?

_____

_____

_____

_____

Tip #3 Mindfulness

Most people will try to heal exclusively by going to the doctor, taking prescribed medications or having surgery, making slight changes to the diet and maybe adding an exercise program. This alone is not enough, and is the reason why so many people get frustrated and don't heal. Although it may become very important to seek a healer, detox the diet and move the energy in your body in order to feel better, complete wellness requires more. Mindfulness and Tip #4, a spiritual practice, will help you truly self-heal and shift energy at a very deep level of your being.

The way we shift and heal an illness is by identifying core wounds. We must close our eyes and connect with the breath as we move into stillness. This act of self-discovery is not easy, and in fact, some people really struggle with this life-saving task. Let's face it, we feel guilty as we sit aimlessly staring into space with groceries to buy, kids screaming and a huge pile of laundry waiting.

For some, it is scary to let go of all the distracting thoughts in our minds. However, our inner world plays such an important role in our health. Few people understand this connection and forget to make room for this ritual. Instead, we would rather complain to a friend, worry needlessly or become depressed. The time has come to close your eyes, shift the energy around old wounds and self-heal.

I like to teach <u>stillness</u>, <u>mindfulness</u> and <u>meditation</u> as three separate disciplines. When broken down, it is not so overwhelming and much safer. When I ask people to meditate, whew––all kinds of concerns are immediately brought to my attention. The question most asked is, "Am I doing it right?" Followed by, "Should I go to a weeklong silent retreat or ashram in India?" To which I promptly reply, "no." It would be like running a marathon without any training. For most women, it would be too much, too fast for the body and mind to safely handle. Begin with sitting still, because it is an easy concept to grasp. There is no right or wrong with stillness. It is simple: sit down, close your eyes and breathe.

After a woman masters being still without interruptions for about 5-10 minutes, it is time to move on to mindfulness. Mindfulness is not meditation, so it also creates limited concerns for most students. We close our eyes and ask the body, emotions and the unconscious mind to identify themselves for the purpose of healing unresolved issues that may be keeping us sick or uncomfortable in our bodies. This process can be long, tedious and a lot of work, but in the end, self-healing is highly likely.

Stepping into mindfulness is a bit different than stillness. By the time you are ready to embrace mindfulness, you are able to sit still for at least 10 minutes without being overwhelmed. Stillness has taught you well, and it is time to advance. In this mindful-state you are aware of your life at a much deeper level and you will find yourself sitting uninterrupted for 10-30 minutes at a time.

As you connect to the supernatural highway at higher speeds, bypassing stillness, you will begin to notice that life's problems are magically being solved, wounds are healed and the heart has mended.

You have changed. When you miss daily mindfulness sessions, you feel out of sorts and unsettled. With time, the mindfulness practice will take you to unknown places of great peace.

As with stillness, edginess will appear from time to time, as wounds are revealed and released. In mindfulness, you learn to become the witness. At this stage, a level of awareness exists that honors the duality between you the witness and your inner world. This is an important piece of the mindfulness practice.

After mastering stillness and mindfulness techniques, it is now time to embrace meditation, or the journey to enlightenment. In this case, enlightenment means great happiness and joy. You will naturally flow into this state without wondering if it is time to move forward or if you are doing it right. Time has no relevance now, as you connect with feelings of joy. Before you know it, you will have created an inner playground to strengthen your aura and balance your chakras. You are the master over a chaotic mind, out-of-control sexual urges and emotional breakdowns. Balance has been restored, and you have become a rock-steady, peaceful woman.

In every religion, there is a form of meditation. Christians, Hindus, Buddhists, Taoists and Native Americans all have specific methods to best serve them. In Transcendental meditation, founded by Maharishi Mahesh Yogi, the student is presented a personalized mantra to be repeated during meditation. A mantra is a prayer or sequence of words that are chanted repetitively. The rhythm of the chant calms the body and mind. After a period of time, a mantra creates a trance-like feeling and an opening for a greater connection into the spirit world.

Zen Buddhism, known for seated meditation, is also a journey to enlightenment. Thinking or fantasizing are treated as intruders and distractions from the aspect of being, and are discouraged by teachers. This sensory-perceptive experience provides the groundwork for a mode of consciousness described as non-dualistic, timeless and a nonverbal connection with oneness or source energy.

As you progress, sitting for periods in excess of an hour tends to be easily welcomed. Deep-seated meditations offered at weeklong silent retreats can be life altering. Non-ordinary states of consciousness can be the outcome of this dedicated method, but are by no means limited to a meditation practice.

Meditation will completely open you up to living a spiritual life, as it lets the spirit world know you are available to play. You can expect to experience spiritual glimpses, or early stages of Samadhi or Christ consciousness, from time-to-time. Having a good teacher to guide you is the key to a successful experience. In the end, a seasoned meditator will tell you it is not how long you are able to sit every day that matters. Life now becomes a living, moment-to-moment meditation.

Can you find time to sit once a day and if not, why?

_____

_____

_____

_____

Where are you currently on your journey: stillness, mindfulness or meditation?

_____

_____

_____

_____

Tip #4 Spiritual practice

In these unsettling times, it is critical to have a daily spiritual practice. Hands down, it is one of the most important regular routines for your well-being. As mentioned, most women would not consider a spiritual practice a necessary protocol for good health and healing, but I have seen first hand the power of rituals. Having a strong connection with the spirit world is very comforting in times of need. Knowing you are supported by a strong nonvisible-force can change the dynamics of your life. It is time to add a customized spiritual practice, one perfect for your lifestyle.

There are no rules when it comes to praying, doing yoga, introspective work, anointing yourself with spiritual essential oils (Palo Santo, Exodus II and Frankincense), reading a sacred book, lighting candles, listening to spiritual music, chanting, dancing, going to a sacred place of worship or talking to the angels. The point is that you just have to do it. It has to be an act that is in line with your higher self. It is so important to know who you are and why you are here on the earth plane. You need to become familiar with your personal style and what type of spiritual practice would best serve your life. Start to ask yourself, "Who am I?"

I have worked with many people in the past. Some of them could have avoided a terrible turn of events in life if they only had had a spiritual practice. I will guarantee you if you don't have a daily practice before you get sick, after you have survived the soul's healing process you will. A life with a strong spiritual connection will become precious to you. Your friends and family will start to notice the changes. A spiritual practice becomes a valuable part of each day. Now when asked, "Who am I?" You will hear an inner answer, "I am thou" (you are the sacred). You have joined forces with the spirit world to become part of a higher vibration where an illness loses its power.

A health problem means spiritual growth is on its way. If you can learn to treat these healing episodes as a sign to go within and ask for guidance, there is a good chance you will recover sooner than later. Struggling with the condition at hand will only make life worse. Control is no longer useful. Hating yourself or God is not an option when going through a healing crisis. A solid spiritual practice is critical along with a wise spiritual teacher who has also experienced a healing crisis, gone through a self-healing process and survived.

When we think of supporting our health, right away we think of going to the doctor for a *check-up*. That is great, but far too often we forget the importance of our own internal *check-in*. My personal healing crisis showed me that all four of the healing tips above are very much needed to heal from a disease and live a quality, healthy life.

It does take an incredible amount discipline, but having your health back and feeling good in your body is well worth this challenge. Once you have experienced self-healing, you will understand what it takes to restore balance. This empowers a lifetime of great health.

What personal beliefs do you have about a spiritual practice?

_____

_____

_____

Do you currently have a spiritual practice? List the benefits below.

_____

_____

_____

_____

Do you have a spiritual teacher?

_____

_____

Teatime Tune-Ups

Get Still——Inquire Actively——Live Consciously

Sit cross-legged, close your eyes and begin to connect with your sacred breath (5 minutes). Stretch your legs out and lightly tap on the outer and inner parts of the legs. Now come back to the cross-legged position. Extend your arms straight out from your chest. Close your right hand into a fist and wrap your left hand around it. Let the base of your palms touch. Your thumbs are touching and sticking up into the air. Place your gaze there. Inhale slowly for 5 counts, exhale for 5 counts and hold the breath out for 15 counts, then continue the inhales and exhales for 2 minutes. Over time, work your way up to 11 minutes. When finished, go into a meditation and then rest.

Health benefits

This teatime tune-up is an antidote to depression and will boost your energy.

Reflect once again on the healing practices above. Do you have any additional personal beliefs or prejudices around this conscious contemplation?

TEA PARTY III

Teatime Tip: *Sit in a comfortable position and take a few deep inhales and exhales. Find a place of inner peace.*

Sample Menu

*Organic Apple Pie warm from the oven
Served with
a dab of cinnamon ice cream*

*Yerba Maté
Served in Hollow Calabash Gourds
Sip through a Metal Straw
&
Sage Tea*

*Conscious Contemplation
Religious and Spiritual Health*

*Teatime Tune-Ups
Step into your True Essence by Designing
Your Inner World*

Recipe

Apple Pie

Ingredients

4-5 medium-size, baking apples: Granny Smith, Fuji or Jonagold
½ teaspoon ground cinnamon
2 drops cinnamon bark essential oil
2 drops clove essential oil
2 drops nutmeg essential oil
½ cup ghee
1 cup agave syrup
½ cup ground flaxseeds
½ cup spelt flour
2 teaspoons baking powder
2 teaspoons vanilla
2 medium eggs, whipped
Pinch sea salt

Preparation

Preheat oven 375 degrees Fahrenheit.

Peel and slice apples into small wedges. Place into a greased pie dish and sprinkle the apples with ground cinnamon and set aside.

In a mixing bowl combine the ghee and agave. Fold in eggs and essential oils then add ground flaxseeds, spelt four, baking powder, salt, vanilla. Mix by hand or use an electric beater until smooth. Pour the mixture over the apples.

Bake for 40 minutes or until brown. Serve warm from the oven and top with cinnamon/vanilla ice cream.

Tea

Yerba Maté

The Guarani originally discovered yerba maté, however it was an order of Catholic priests, the Jesuits, who are responsible for its international popularity. Maté is typically served in a hollow calabash gourd with a metal straw. This tea contains high levels of polyphenol antioxidants and vitamins: A, C, E, B1, B2, Niacin (B3), B5 and B Complex. Maté has an abundance of minerals like calcium, iron, selenium, potassium, magnesium, phosphorus and zinc. Serve this tea hot or cold and sip all day long.

Optional essential oil: add two drops of Frankincense into your infusion. This essential oil is known to support the body when it is in pain.

Conscious Contemplation

Religious and Spiritual Health

Conscious tea parties offer an ideal setting for examining our religious and spiritual beliefs. From time to time, it is important to find peace and calm by checking in with ourselves. Ask yourself if religious views are affecting your life in a positive or negative way.

As we get beyond limiting beliefs and prejudices, we are ready to understand the meaning of consciousness at a much deeper level.

The sole (soul) purpose of this review is to provide an opportunity to reflect on religious beliefs and any prejudices that may be blocking a deeper spiritual evolution and good health. If thinking about or discussing a world religion causes you to become emotionally unhinged, this is a powerful sign that there is work to be done. It is time to examine the agitation and silent prejudices that lie somewhere unresolved deep within the body. If any religious or spiritual choices other than your own are daunting, try to understand why. These charged emotions block spiritual advancements and limit inner peace.

Key Point

In order for sophisticated women to come together for a mystical conversation at a Conscious Afternoon Tea, there must be a common platform from which to launch. In other words, we need to be on the same page. When spirituality is discussed, most of us tend to go right back in our minds to our religious upbringing. This may impede learning a greater spiritual message. Major world religions offer spiritual truths during times of need. Then it is up to our inner true selves to go deeper into higher levels of consciousness to spiritually connect with God, source energy or the great oneness of the non-dual.

What does all this mean? Your spiritual journey could force you to re-evaluate your religious beliefs. Your perspective on religious dogmas and ancient texts might have shifted over the years. You might have outgrown the religious stories of your childhood. Maybe it is time to expand your devotion instead of focusing on just one religious tradition.

A conscious spiritual conversation at a tea party is less based on religion and is instead deeply related to discovering the mystic within. To grow spiritually means to have a greater personal connection with the spirit world, God, Allah or source energy. It might even mean experiencing a non-ordinary state of consciousness. These new experiences will teach us how to go beyond fear, anger, aggression or any conflicting emotion that overtakes love.

Today, women seek greater religious freedom. We demand more meaning out of life, with added love and less fear. We want to liberate ourselves from the chains of oppression as we explore our spiritual selves. The unrest in the world may have a lot to do with the masses waking up to seek truth and freedom. It is our duty to access religious and spiritual components like prayer, contemplation and meditation, even if it means dancing with the Sufis. Our responsibility is to form a deeper relationship with spirit, then share this love out in the world.

Some of us spend a lifetime in search of a religious or spiritual practice, while others may stay true to the way they were raised and never question their religion's dogmas. One might ask, do we truly have *free will* when it comes to our spiritual choices and religious prejudices? Or has our soul come into this world preset on a specific human-spirit vibration? This is certainly a profound question to contemplate at a Conscious Afternoon Tea.

There are many religious and spiritual paths these days. Nine of the most popular religions that come to mind are: Christianity, Islam, Hinduism, Buddhism, Folk, Sikhism, Judaism and Baha'ism. A wise teacher shared that there are around 21 formal religions in the world today. Once we understand the magnificence of this, we can start to make new choices. The majority of women still seek religion for peace when life gets difficult. Religions and spiritual practices are not going away anytime soon, although major changes are brewing.

Throughout my studies, I have discovered that most religions once started with a mystical, spiritual experience. For my own personal journey, this was a key realization. The words *spiritual truth* and *religion* are often intermingled. This was confusing then one day it became clear. Organized religions grew out of a personal spiritual experience or an altered state of awareness in order to be actualized onto this earth plane. So in the end, to be religious or spiritual should bring forth love that leads us into deeper levels of consciousness.

Since the beginning of time, some religions have set out to control and block our deeper inner journeys. History has revealed some shocking instances that have occurred in the name of religion. If we are going to value and trust institutionalized religions once again, we must try hard to see old truths in a different way. By not rejecting institutional religions completely, there is a chance to awaken their fundamental truths in today's world. Maybe then more people could get back on board with a religion or spiritual community that is heading to a higher level of consciousness.

In the end, it is about enhancing love and eliminating fear. Seek only love.

Important Definitions:

An Agnostic is one who claims that the existence of God(s) is unknowable.

An Atheist is one who lacks a belief in God(s).

A Freethinker is one who forms opinions (usually in the context of religion) on the basis of reasons independent of any authority.

A Religious person strongly adheres to the dogma of a particular faith and usually attends a specific place of worship of that same belief.

A Spiritual woman believes in God, a higher power or Divine spirits. She might avoid a church, temple or other specific places of worship. At times being at the ocean, in the woods, watching a sunset or listening to beautiful music at home are sacred opportunities to feel the Divine. Also this woman might not welcome deeper states of consciousness or mystical experiences.

Spiritual Mystics, Buddhists and Yoginis seek freedom through a deep experience in altered states. The seeker comes to knows, "I and the observer of the I" as duality. The seeker continues deeper on the journey to establish a profound connection with universal *oneness* or the non-dual. Systems like Advaita Vedanta in Hinduism or Zen and Dzogchen in Buddhism encourage entering the non-dual. These systems help create a love vortex with a spiritual force that overcome the illusion of separation.

In some tea parties, I have seen that when words like spirituality, consciousness and mystical gifts are mentioned, eyes tend to gloss over and women start to squirm in their seats. I can't express enough how important it is to accept the past and not be afraid to clear old ideas from your mind. Learn to be open and accepting of new behaviors. It will serve you highly in the future. Trust the universe and breathe into the fear of the unknown.

Close your eyes and focus on your inhale and exhale. What personal beliefs do you have about religion, spirituality and seeking deeper level of consciousness? Describe.

_____

_____

_____

_____

Where in your body are you holding negative beliefs regarding religion? Describe.

_____

_____

_____

_____

Do you consider yourself religious, spiritual or neither? Describe.

_____

_____

_____

_____

How does experiencing deeper levels of consciousness relate to your current religious or spiritual journey?

_____

_____

_____

_____

Teatime Tune-Ups

Get Still––Inquire Actively––Live Consciously

Sit cross-legged, close your eyes and begin to connect with your sacred breath. After about 2 minutes, uncross your legs and spread them apart as far as you can. Sit with a straight spine. You might need to sit on a pillow to support your body. Clasp your hands behind your back (or grab elbows) and inhale deeply, exhale, drop your head to your left knee and allow the hands to go over your head as far as possible. When your head is down chant, "HAR" and when you come up say, "HARAY." Drop your head to the other leg, and continue. *Har* means cosmic reality and *Haray* means God projected.

After 2 minutes, change the pattern. Continue the exercise as described above except this time add the center. So the flow is left leg, middle then right leg back to the middle and continue. Note:

inhales and exhales will come naturally while chanting and moving. Finish after 2 minutes and inhale and exhale, folding forward into the center again and stay there with your legs extended. If you can reach your toes, then wrap your first two fingers around your big toes. Hold for a minute then exhale up. Meditate in a seated position then lie down to rest.

Health benefits

This healing ritual balances the lower spine, helps ease constipation, the pain of arthritis and improves eyesight.

Reflect once again on the conscious contemplation above. Notice if any other personal beliefs or prejudices have now surfaced.

_____

_____

_____

_____

TEA PARTY IV

Teatime Tip: *Offer tea to your girlfriends as if it was a life-alternating gift.*

Sample Menu

Sun Kissed Organic Peach Cobbler

Milky Oolong Tea
&
Cinnamon Spice Tea

Conscious Contemplation
Yoga

Teatime Tune-Ups
Regenerate the Nervous System
Peacefully Grounded

Recipe

Peach Cobbler

Ingredients

Crumb topping
1 cup spelt flour
1 cup flaxseed flour

1 cup raw steel oats
Pinch sea salt
2 drops cinnamon essential oil
¼ cup ghee
½ cup agave syrup
¼ cup raw hazelnuts, chopped
¼ cup raw and sprouted almonds, chopped

Peach filling

5 cups diced fresh peaches
½ cup wolfberries
2 drops cinnamon essential oil
2 drops nutmeg essential oil,
1 cup agave syrup

Preparation

The night before, sprout the almonds. Place raw almonds in a glass jar and add purified water to cover. Let sit overnight and rinse in the morning. Add the nuts to a pot of boiling water for one minute. Rinse with cold water. The brown skin of the almond can now be easily removed. Shuck the almonds and chop in blender or food processor.

Note: in any of the recipes that call for nuts, feel free to sprout. It is easy to do and offers many benefits: more nutrients, increased enzymes and easier to digest.

Preheat oven to 350 degree Fahrenheit.

In a large mixing bowl, combine ingredients for the topping and set aside.

In a second mixing bowl, add cut peaches, wolfberries and essential oils. Fill individual ramekins ½ of the way with filling and top with crumb topping. Bake for 10 minutes.

Tea

Milky Oolong

I was first introduced to Milky Oolong in Germany. The owner of a delightful, local teashop in Frankfurt told me it was by far her favorite tea, and ever since, I have been introducing others to this sweet, velvety infusion. Milky Oolong is a hand-processed tea grown in the Fujian mountains in China. As hot water is poured over the rolled leaves, the tea begins to emit an irresistible creamy aroma. Oolong is made from the leaves, buds and stems of black and green tea, making it partially fermented (black tea) and unfermented (green tea).

Oolong tea seems to improve your mood and calm the nerves. It is thought to have qualities that help prevent heart disease, diabetes, cancer and osteoporosis. Oolong tea has also been used to treat obesity and skin allergies. Some say it is the perfect tea for supporting the immune system. It is truly a tea you can consume all day without feeling over caffeinated.

Optional essential oil: add a couple drops of Lavender oil to this infusion. Lavender is an anti-inflammatory.

Conscious Contemplation

Yoga

The word yoga means union. This integration is represented when a person finds universal oneness with God or source energy through enlightenment. The breathing aspect of yoga represents this personal unification with the spirit world. The deep inhales and exhales actually clear the mind and transform the body, allowing the yoga movements (asanas) to become a deep meditation. Yoga soon becomes a life-altering dance with the mystical realm.

I would like to share a short story from my past. This is a very significant tale for me as a yoga teacher. It is truly one of the reasons behind my writing this book and it goes something like this:

The evening yoga class was just about to begin. All the students were in their proper places and stood strong at the head of their sticky mats. Hands were at the heart in Namaste, and the Hindu invocation was just about to commence when all of a sudden a little whimper came from the middle of the studio. "I can't say this prayer; it is against my religion."

The room filled with an awkward silence. The students were anxiously waiting for me to respond. At the time, my comment back to the young yogini was quite civil. I

immediately accepted her religious beliefs, in spite of the
fact it felt like a lack of respect for the Hindu's sacred yogi
prayer and the other yoga students in the class.

Unforeseen at the time, this student's comment
would linger, staying unresolved in the cells of my heart
for almost 25 years. I was truly grateful that the yogini
felt safe enough in class to express her concern. Yet, I was
confused how a person could partake in a religious teaching
like yoga (a Hindu religion) and not honor its religious
origin? How can prejudice or religious fears still exist in
the 21st century? How can one religion still make claims
that they are better than another or place restrictions on
the members of their spiritual communities? Inner peace
and maybe even world peace might come from resolving
some of these powerful questions.

The *Conscious Afternoon Teas* book all began
with a yoga class, a simple prayer and my
personal interest to help women expand their
spiritual lives.

The more conscious we become, the more we can share a peaceful
existence with others and ourselves. Nothing is more frustrating than
trying to have a spiritual conversation with religious interruptions.
As mentioned before, often when we hear the word *spiritual*, our
minds immediately run back to our religious upbringing. In the
end, we often fail to understand the greater mystical opportunity
being presented.

Presently, in the Western world, we don't often consider yoga
to be a form of religion or spirituality. It is regarded by many as
a healthy method for stretching, and basic form of exercise. As a
person becomes more evolved, it is easier to see outside this limited
perception.

In India, yoga has always been revered as a sacred way of life and part of an ancient religion. Yoga has played a key role in defining higher states of consciousness. It is only within the last couple of decades that the West has turned the primordial, world religion of yoga into a trendy, *power* workout.

After the class in the story above, the yoga student privately shared with me that when she was asked to pray, it really challenged her religious beliefs. She truly had no idea yoga could be anything other than an exercise program, and her Christian religion restricted her from participating in other religious prayers or rituals. Without judging the young student's passage as right or wrong, let's open our hearts and minds. I guess it is time to serve *tea*...

Originally yoga was practiced as a sacred ritual, a way to prepare the body for a spiritual awakening. It was not the pursuit of physical fitness. Incredible things can be done with the body, but this has little to do with enlightenment or spiritual advancements. If the ego takes charge with a desire to show off, this can actually impede spiritual growth.

There are four main yoga traditions in the Hindu religion. These practices are the following: Jnana Yoga or the way to God through knowledge, Bhakti Yoga or the way to God through love, Karma Yoga or the way to God through work and Raja Yoga or the way to God through psychophysical movement.

The famous Hatha yoga, a psychophysical style, has made its way to the West and offers asanas (postures) to detox the body, emotions and mind as it opens us up to a greater connection to the spirit realm. Hatha yoga addresses the gross or physical body. The breath and movements over time can stir a sleeping force within us. This spiritual awakening arouses a serpent-like energy that weaves up the spine (Sushumna) to the crown of head, then back down to the heart. As this energy gets activated, it clears old traumatic imprints, and opens our psychic centers or chakras. Based on the karmic information and soul contracts that live inside of you, this can be a very powerful experience.

Keep in mind, this energy moves regardless of where you are in the moment. You might be in a yoga class, making love or at the grocery store. A spiritual awakening is not attached to a spiritual practice like yoga or meditation. Instead, consider it a rite of passage available for all of us to experience at certain times in our lives. This internal movement of energy is called Kundalini Rising. The Sanskrit word, *kunda* means coiled, and any style of yoga safely prepares the body, mind, emotions and soul for this profound unraveling of energy.

Kundalini Rising is a spiritual awakening that helps the nervous system relinquish excess stress, removes blocked energy, changes the blood and awakens consciousness. Kundalini has many names: Holy Spirit, Grace, Skekhinah, Anima, Chi, Bodhicitta. It is the subtle body that describes universal consciousness. This energy flow is also known by the Sanskrit name Mumukshtva, or longing for liberation. The entire process is one of purification and should not be feared.

Everyone's Kundalini Rising will be extremely different. This is truly a solo journey. I will say that my personal experiences have been quite gentle. I have had my moments with the extraordinary, but as long as I stay grounded, do my yoga, watch my diet, pray and meditate, I feel pretty secure when shifts of deep healing come along. A healthy diet of spirituality is key to a safe rising experience. My personal belief is that Kundalini Rising shifts will continue throughout a lifetime or until the death of our physical bodies. Which in my opinion is the final and most important spiritual awakening. Remember these shifts in consciousness help us expand and grow, and should be considered a fundamental part of the human experience here on earth.

We often consider a spiritual practice, like yoga or meditation, as a tool to force a Kundalini Rising experience. I found this is not always the case. Any health problem or life change can be considered the onset of a stirred up Kundalini. My clients have shown me that their healing crises have served as profound death and rebirth processes in their lives. They were able to rebirth their old dysfunctional selves into a new existence. In some cases, women shifted so much I barely recognized them with their weight loss and facial changes.

I've successfully helped my clients address Kundalini risings with many methods, including yoga, a modification in diet, meditation for balancing the chakra energies, some exercise and energy medicine. This approach has helped to create a gentle spiritual awakening experience for many who were going through this amazing transformational shift.

Kundalini Yoga

Kundalini Yoga is a specific style of yoga and should not to be confused with a Kundalini Rising experience. This yoga is also a psychophysical style that aligns and clears the energy of the body in preparation for a deep spiritual opening. Kundalini Yoga can activate a creative inner feminine force called, Adi Shakti and addresses the subtle (astral or etheric) energy bodies.

The rigorous and sometimes intense movements performed in a Kundalini Yoga class resemble the actions one might experience when going through a spiritual awakening. Deep, long breathing balances the nervous and endocrine systems, opens the lungs, and improves the lymphatic and cardio circulation. Movements called kriyas are predetermined combinations of pranayama (deep breathing), mudras (hand movement), mantras (sacred chants), asanas (postures), dhrist (eye focus) and meditation that gently open the physical realm to receive a higher spiritual vibration. In the end, Kundalini yoga helps to balance the Shakti (feminine) and Shiva (masculine) energies within us.

For centuries, this style had been kept a secret and could only be obtained from a guru. In the late 60s, a teacher by the name of Yogi Bhajan came to the West to offer this transformative style of yoga to all seekers. Unfortunately, many people are still labeling Kundalini Yoga as dangerous. This is a myth.

The power of Kundalini Yoga comes from looking at our physical energy as separate subtle bodies. This concept helps yogis get a better sense of where the energy is being balanced when specific kriyas are performed. This takes yoga to a new level and it is no longer appropriate to think of it as just a form of stretching.

The following is a list of eleven subtle bodies used in Kundalini Yoga:

- *The Soul Body* is the Divine aspect of our Self
- *The Negative Mind* defines who we are by knowing who we are not
- *The Positive Mind* is our positive aspect or seeing the positive in life
- *The Neutral Mind* is the state of non-attachment
- *The Physical Body* is teacher of balance between spiritual and physical/emotional
- *The Arc Line* is the power of prayer
- *The Aura* is our personal vibration, a sphere of electro-magnetic energy
- *The Pranic Body* connects us to the life force of infinity
- *The Subtle Body* offers a conscious journey between worlds
- *The Radiant Body* provides the ability to radiate a benevolent power
- *The Embodiment* is spiritual commitment

I had been studying Asthanga and Iyengar Yoga for about 21 years before embracing Kundalini Yoga. I will never forget my first experience, which was at a Yoga Journal convention in Estes Park, Colorado. The early morning Kundalini Yoga class, called Sadhana, began promptly at 4:00 a.m. The room was packed with a sea of people, all wearing white clothing. There was live music in the background as people gently settled down and closed their eyes to begin the practice.

I found myself stepping out of my ego and competitive nature, into an energy force in line with the spirit world. Since the practice is done with eyes closed, there is an immediately connection to God. I felt I had found the yoga that could lead me to the next level on my spiritual quest. The most lasting impression was when I stepped out of class. As I looked out at the trees, I could see auric vibrations around the elements with bursts of intense colors. The park became alive, and it felt like I was floating on another realm of consciousness. It was very powerful.

Be prepared for a safe spiritual connection, a strong chakra system, a healthy aura and much more when practicing Kundalini Yoga.

Personally, I have never met a Kundalini Yoga student who has gone through a dangerous Kundalini Rising experience. As a yoga instructor, I don't teach students to do yoga to stimulate a spiritual awakening. We do the practice to prepare our bodies for when our awakening occurs. In the end, Kundalini Yoga, when practiced safely, opens the body to receive a gentle awakening and transforms tension in the body into spiritual energy. If you are already a yogini committed to another style of yoga, try adding Kundalini Yoga once a week. It will definitely compliment a spiritual journey.

The following are honored chants or mantras used in Kundalini Yoga:

- Ang Sang Wahey Guru (God is present in every cell in my body)
- Ong Namo Guru Dev Namo (I bow to the Divine Channel of Wisdom)
- Ek Ong Kar (One Creator created Creation)
- Sat Nam (The Truth is My Name)

- Sa Ta Na Ma (Infinity, Life, Death, Rebirth)
- Har Haray (Cosmic reality and God projected)

> *He who does the task*
> *Dictated by duty*
> *Caring nothing*
> *For the fruit of the action,*
> *He is a yogi.*
> (Bhagavad-Gita, VI:I)

The Ashtanga Yoga Invocation
(The prayer that was against my student's religion)

OM
Vande Gurunam Caranaravinde,
(I bow to the lotus feet of the Gurus)
Sandarsita Svatma Sukhava Bodhe,
(The awakening happiness of one's own Self-revealed)
Nih Sreyase Jangalikayamane,
(Beyond better acting like the jungle physician)
Samsara Halahala Mohasantyai,
(Pacifying delusion, the poison of Samsara)
Abahu Purusakaram,
(Taking the form of a man to the shoulders)
Sankhacakrasi Dharinam,
(Holding a conch, a discus and a sword)
Sahasra Sirasam Svetam,
(One thousand heads, white)
Pranamami Patanjalim
(To Patanjali, I salute)

What personal beliefs do you have about yoga as a religion?

_____

_____

_____

_____

What are your beliefs about Kundalini Yoga?

_____

_____

_____

_____

Teatime Tune-Ups

Get Still—Inquire Actively—Live Consciously

Sit cross-legged, close your eyes and begin to connect with your sacred breath (5 minutes). Stretch out your legs for a moment (stand if necessary) then come back to a seated cross-legged position. Bend your right arm and hold your right hand at your ear. Touch your thumb to the ring finger. Place the left hand in your lap with the tip of the thumb touching the little finger. Breathe deeply with long, even breaths. Make sure your spine remains straight and your gaze is soft, either with eyes closed looking at the middle of the forehead or slightly opened and looking at tip of your nose. Practice holding this position for 11 minutes and try to work up to 31 minutes. When finished, inhale, raise the arms overhead and shake them rapidly. Then relax.

Health benefits

This meditation supports the nervous system. When life gets rough, this meditation will protect you from becoming irrational and reactive.

Reflect once again on the spiritual practice of yoga. Notice if any new personal beliefs, fears or prejudices have now surfaced.

_____

_____

_____

_____

TEA PARTY V

Teatime Tip: *Let the warmth of the tea soothe your body and open the heart.*

Sample Menu

Wolfberry Cheesecake
Topped with a NingXia Red Strawberry Sauce

Fresh Mint Leaf Tea from the Garden

Conscious Contemplation
Energy Hygiene

Teatime Tune-Ups
Discover Inner Gifts of the
Open Heart

Recipe

Wolfberry Cheesecake

Ingredients

Crust
1 cup almonds, ground
¾ cup walnuts, ground
½ cup hazelnuts, ground
¼ cup maple syrup
½ cup ghee

Filling

1ˢᵗ Layer
48 ounces quark or cream cheese
8 eggs whites, beaten stiff
2 cups agave syrup
2 teaspoons vanilla
½ cup goji berries

2ⁿᵈ layer
2 cups plain yogurt
2 tablespoons agave syrup
1 teaspoon vanilla extract

Topping

3 cups fresh strawberries
½ cup maple syrup
½ cup Young Living's NingXia Red Juice

Preparation

Preheat oven to 325 degrees Fahrenheit.

Finely grind nuts in a food processor. *Almonds and walnuts can be sprouted the nights before like in the previous recipe. Hazelnuts do not need sprouting.* Mix with agave and ghee. In a greased 9-inch spring-form pan, place the nut mixture and use the palm of your hand to form a crust.

1ˢᵗ Layer

Blend the quark or cream cheese with agave and vanilla. In a separate bowl, beat the egg whites. Fold the whites into the cheese. Add the goji berries, stirring gently to distribute. Pour the mixture into the crust. Bake for an hour. After an hour, turn off the oven and leave the cheesecake in for an additional 30 minutes. Remove from oven, and cool in the refrigerator for 20 minutes.

2*nd* Layer

Mix the yogurt, vanilla and agave. Place the mixture on top of chilled cheesecake. Bake at 375 degree Fahrenheit for 15 minutes. Allow cake to cool completely before removing the ring from the pan.

Topping

In a blender, puree all the ingredients. Chill. Drizzle over cheesecake before serving.

Tea

Mint Tea

To make garden mint tea, simply place fresh mint leaves into hot water. Mint has sedative, disinfectant and anti-inflammatory properties. This herb has been successfully used for gastro-intestinal disorders. It supports the liver and calms indigestion. It is also recommended in cases of asthma, bronchitis and the flu because of its antispasmodic and sedative properties.

For an extra treat, add a few slices of fresh ginger and the juice of a lime. The ginger supports digestion while the lime helps boost the immune system.

Optional essential oil: add a couple of drops of Geranium oil to the infusion. Internally this oil can be a diuretic and used to detox the body. It may help to release negative memories.

Conscious Contemplation

Energy Hygiene

In recent years, energy hygiene has become a very important topic for discussion. When you step onto a spiritual path, you become very sensitive as your energy shifts to higher states of consciousness and your intuitive gifts are revealed. You remain acutely aware of your human egoic self where emotions like fear, unworthiness and anger are on high alert.

At the same time, you begin to acknowledge a Divine sweetness and peaceful presence. It takes time to embody wholeness, so opportunities come along to help us interlace these two paradoxical parts of our being. The question now becomes, what can you do to keep your human side balanced and safe as you embark upon a spiritual lifestyle? What do you need to know?

Sensitivity

Metaphysically, we are all getting much more savvy when it comes to energy, our own and others'. Being empathetic means you can deeply feel the energy of your surroundings. As women, we can easily feel another person's pain. Being empathetic means you can actually feel another person's imbalances inside your own body. Next time you walk into a room and start feeling overwhelmed, ask yourself, "Is this my energy or the lady's standing next to me?"

When you feel sad, disturbed or anxious, don't assume it is always your own emotion. You may be picking up someone else's energy. Some people's life force will drain you, while other people are wonderful to be around and are even uplifting. True empaths can find it harsh to be in busy places filled with crowds of people. Loud noises and brightly colored lights are very disturbing. Overly abusive and critical family members can literally drain an empath of their life force.

Sensitive, healthy women are not naïve about the work that must be done in order to grow spiritually. Along the way, there are hurdles in the human experience that must be overcome. As we set forth to transcend into whole beings, our shadow, or the not so pretty sides of ourselves, will emerge. This is a major part of the human experience. Our shadow is not evil. It helps us to see the harsh emotions that live within us. These feelings must be welcomed and healed. Our shadow side can actually be a gift. As we take the time to go within, reflect and shift our inner wounds, we are energetically affecting others in the world.

On the journey to wholeness, we sometimes get caught up in a struggle with lower vibrations. We need to be aware of what is happening to our energy. As sensitive, intuitive creatures, we are going to feel various emotions. In order for us not to get overwhelmed by these feelings, we need to learn how to *consciously shelter* ourselves as we continue upon our spiritual paths.

Some of us might become victims of people who steal our energy. These energy snatchers come into our life to show us our weaknesses or shadow wounds. Many of us may have gotten into an unhealthy habit of feeding off of other people's energy to feel good, instead of doing the important spiritual work ourselves. This is why a discussion on energy hygiene is so important. Until we can fully transcend into our spiritual selves, we must stay focused on healing our shadow selves. If not, it will be difficult to have healthy human relationships.

In the West, we are obsessed with being clean. We take showers twice a day, even when we aren't dirty. Our clothes must always be clean and tidy. Poor hygiene is not tolerated, and in fact, it is considered a sign of weakness or a lower economic class in our society. Unfortunately, the same isn't true about our energy hygiene.

Good energy hygiene means we consciously take responsibility for our personal life force. We avoid numbing ourselves and stay present with our daily interactions. Poor hygiene can translate into unresolved emotions of our shadow selves. This can create a negative force in the world, as we unconsciously hook into another person's energy to feel pleasure or power. We may also allow other people to hook into our energy due to early childhood abuse and feelings of unworthiness.

Human Energy Vampires or lower frequencies exist, and as we transcend this shadow within ourselves, we are able to shift the energy around us. Today, with the major surge of sensitive, spiritual women coming into the world, it is critical that we clearly understand this concept and the ramifications this will have to our human experience.

Here is a short personal story I thought you might enjoy and should illustrate the point quite well:

> About four years ago, I attend a workshop at a popular healing center in upstate New York. My husband and I had joined a class geared toward owning a healing center. After the first session was over, it was dinnertime, so off we went to the café. I had befriended a girl earlier that day. She joined us for dinner, which turned out to be a blessing in disguise.
>
> I was the first to get my meal and went off to secure seating for my hubby and new friend. As I sat down at an abandoned table in the middle of this huge dining room, I energetically started to connect with the café. I was sending out my energy in hopes of locating my husband. Right away a man clear across the room locked eyes with me. I literally saw fangs come out of his mouth as he flew across the room to sit at my table, directly across from me.

Okay, maybe I had been watching too much Vampire Diary TV during my free time. In any case, the man was hooking into my energy as he quietly sat staring at me. It was quite obvious to me because I could actually feel him in my solar plexus with a painful, overwhelming force. It literally took my breath away.

When my new friend joined me, she immediately saw that the nice vampire man was sucking my energy dry. By now, I could barely talk but I managed to ask the guy what workshop he was attending. He said, "Oh no, I am not attending a workshop. I live in the neighborhood and I only come here to eat." Of course he did, I thought.

Once my husband joined us, it was pretty clear that we were all being challenged by this man's poor energy hygiene. Hubby kept saying, "Hurry up, let's get out of here" and my friend just shook her head in disappointment. When we finally got away from the table, I was almost unconscious.

My friend took me to the nearest tree and told me to hold on and breathe. Oh brother, I had heard about tree huggers, and that whole thing was not my style. Here I was at a very up-scaled and well-known spiritual center where my energy should be safe from hungry vampire-types. Well, off I went to grab a tree. As soon as I started taking long, deep breaths, I felt much better. The tree and my friend saved me from this extreme energy attack.

After this situation played out, the dynamic of poor energy hygiene became so clear to me. Not only from the man who invaded our table at dinner that night, but also for myself. As a highly sensitive, spiritual woman, I could have done a better job protecting my life force. This man was attracted to my spiritual vibration. Unfortunately, I was unguarded, which made me an easy target and vulnerable to having my energy tapped. It was time to grow by creating stronger personal boundaries. My shadow self in this case helped me understand areas in my life where I still felt unsafe, ungrounded or unworthy.

So let's roll up our sleeves and grow together. The more informed we are, the better we can work with these difficult energy situations. Let's start by defining what it means to "hook" into someone life force. Every one of us from time to time can unconsciously become a vampire and hook into a person's energy. Anytime we interact with someone, our energies get intermingled. If a person hooks in, you may start to suddenly feel tired, foggy or irritated. Energy hooks can be so extreme that you can get violently ill within just minutes.

The opposite is also true. If all of sudden there is an extreme, uplifting shift inside of you then BAM, you might have just hooked into someone's beautiful energy source. You have now become the vampire!.

Victims of energy abuse usually live a life unaware of what is going on. A tip is to notice how you feel. The area in the body most affected when a person gets hooked is the 3rd chakra, or our personal power. You will feel pain or tension in this area if energy has been snagged, and at the same time, you will understand that these deep emotional hooks want your attention. Do keep in mind, people can hook into you anywhere: the back of your neck, chest, hips or legs.

Most of us don't mean to steal a person's energy; we just are not consciously aware we're doing it. We need to learn to be responsible for ourselves and, at the same time, be thoughtful of other's energies. Now more than ever, spiritual women are extremely open and most of the time unguarded and ungrounded. This makes it very hard to notice energy vampires.

Loud and excessive talking is a sure sign that a person is hooking into you. When this happens, immediately stand up and back away from the person. Take your right hand to the pelvis bone and pull it up the front of your body to the bottom of your lower lip. Sweep your body a couple of times and quickly get control of the situation as you ground with deep breaths (below the navel). I have people who hook into me over the phone. I usually sweep my body, and sometimes the only way to protect my God-given life force is to put down the phone or hang up.

Intentional long eye contact, like the man in the story above, is another example of hooking, sometimes called "cording in." Watch out for people who are constantly waving their hands into your energy field or standing too close to you. Immediately, drop any eye contact with these people, move out of the way and sweep your body. Intuitively, send them a message that they are not welcome in your personal space.

If a person needs to show off, this could be a sign of an energy snatcher. If you are sensitive, you will most likely feel them in your solar plexus. My girlfriend was hosting a tea party on my behalf, and the last person to arrive made such a grand "showy" entrance, I immediately thought, *poor energy hygiene.*

As the party transitioned from the food/tea celebration into the sacred ritual, this woman got up abruptly in the middle of the meditation and started to loudly cough as she scuffed noisily off to the bathroom. Now coughing is not necessarily a form of hooking energy, but in this case the woman intentionally broke the silence and the spiritual connection in the room. I could literally see her energetically skimming off the tasty energy of people who were upset by her actions. And yes, if a person upsets you, they have just snagged your energy.

Start to notice people with ungrounded, crazy amounts of energy, and it reasons that they are getting it from somewhere. Upon meeting these types, immediately sweep your body. The woman from the tea party example above was very lively and aggressive. Those two qualities are definitely signs to watch out for when defending your energy from the snatcher types.

If someone says something to purposefully hurt your feelings, they have just knowingly or unknowingly hooked into your energy field. If this happens, sweep your body. If you still feel them or see their face in your mind's eye, this means they are still hooked.

Continue to breath deeply below the navel and envision water at the top of the head flowing down over the entire body to cleanse your aura.

When someone bumps up against you, aggressively touches or yells at you, immediately stand back and get your bearings; they are hooking in to your life force. Ground yourself and sweep. In the late 80s, when I was in computer software sales, I had a boss who would call his sales team in for a quick pump-up before a big business opportunity. The only person getting pumped up was the boss man. He would yell and belittle each of us until he had snagged all of our energies, leaving his prized team high and dry. This was not a good strategy for developing a successful sales force.

In situations like this, the only thing to do is to call in the angels. Ask them to shield you and the other innocent victims. Archangel Michael is known as the "Big Gun" protective force when times get scary. Please remember to call upon this angel's energy in these types of situations. Then afterwards, head to the bathroom to wash your hands (up to your elbows), and clear the energy around your body.

Blame is a big hook and within minutes can drain a person's energy. How many times do we carelessly blame our husbands or children for doing something wrong? This really can suck a lot of life force out of the people we love. Try to improve your energy hygiene, and think twice before placing blame. Even if you are silently blaming someone, there is very good chance that the person will feel the hook. Since we are all interconnected, psychic hooks of blame can be just as harmful. So learn to stop accusing people all together.

When strong negative thoughts arise, they will be followed by an emotional charge. This emotion is full of hurtful energy, and when placed consciously or unconsciously upon another person, will snag their energy. That is why spiritual teachers stress to their students the importance of maintaining a neutral mind. In the neutral space there is no energy charge, resulting in good energy hygiene. When you find yourself dealing with an emotional person, immediately ground and take good care of yourself.

If, in the past, you practiced poor energy hygiene with friends, family and clients, it is time to examine why. As you empower yourself with a new spiritual vibration, the people around you will learn to treat you and your energy differently. You might meet up with some resistance, and in this case, be prepared. This is an opportunity to teach healthy energy hygiene. If you become aware of vampire girlfriends, don't respond emotionally and continue to let them suck your energy; there will be negative consequences. The universe will not reward this type of behavior.

I have been guilty of hooking a person's energy. During an insightful conversation with a student, I may notice an energy shift and my voice deepens. The spirit world has come to use me to channel an important truth. At times, the message being downloaded may be way too personal for the woman to hear. This can overwhelm her and cause much discomfort. I must say, this is not my goal as a healer. This gal may feel as if her energy has been hooked, and indeed it has, only this time from the spirit world.

It has taken a lifetime to realize that I use communication (fifth chakra) to energetically support people. When this happens, I have learned to back off, and unless a woman comes to me directly for a healing session, her energy is off limits.

Grounding

When you are not properly grounded in your body or do not have a healthy relationship with yourself, you become very vulnerable to vampires or to becoming one. Women who were abused or have addictions need to be very careful and learn to stay in their bodies. Spiritual women must pay extra close attention to ground after their morning spiritual practices. If you are a woman who plays the victim role rather well in your relationships, you are bound to get your energy snagged by others.

The universe does a great job pointing out our shadow work by placing certain kinds of people into our surroundings. This is key. If a vampire has hooked you, it is a sign to get busy and do some more healing on core emotional wounds to discover why this happened. Everyday it is highly likely that you will exchange energy with someone. Make sure you are consciously grounding yourself. The easiest way is to take long deep breaths all the way below the navel. At the end of the day, get into the bathtub with sea salt and apple cider vinegar to safely clear your energy. The *Conscious Dinner Parties* book also mentions this method. While in the bath, call your energy back home and release any that you have taken by mistake.

You become ungrounded:

- While watching TV
- Working on the computer
- Driving the car
- Talking on the phone
- Skyping
- Drinking alcohol or doing drugs

You become grounded:

- While eating
- During sex
- With exercise
- In the shower or bath
- Walking along the beach
- Practicing yoga and deep breathing

In order to have good energy hygiene, learn to stay consciously grounded. If you are talking to someone and all of a sudden you start to feel icky, beware of your energy being snatched. Or if you feel a surge of amazing energy, you have probably just taken someone's vital life force, and it is time to return it. Human Energy Vampires will teach you more about the human experience and your shadow self. Assume you will meet one everyday. This way you will not be caught off guard, like I was in my story.

Our human life force is the most precious gift we have been blessed with, and we are its guardians. The more responsible we become for our energy hygiene, the better chance this world will have to shine with love. Developing into a peaceful woman means having a clear understanding of energy, working with your shadow self and getting a good handle on your hygiene.

Quick Recap

- Ground by taking deep breaths below the navel or find a tree to hug (giggle)
- Sweep your body starting at the pelvis bone, going up to your bottom lip
- Call in the angels for protection
- Simply stand up and move away from the person hooking into your energy
- After a stimulating encounter, as you are leaving, mentally say, "I give back energy and reclaim mine."
- Bathe every night and disconnect
- Chant, *Ong Namo Guru Dev Namo* (I bow to the Divine Channel of Wisdom) three times for protection

What personal beliefs do you have about energy hygiene?

_____

_____

_____

_____

Have you ever encountered an energy vampire or are you a vampire?

_____

_____

_____

_____

Teatime Tune-Ups

Get Still––Inquire Actively––Live Consciously

Sit cross-legged, close your eyes and begin to connect with your sacred breath (5 minutes). Stretch your legs and when you are ready, come back to the seated cross-legged position. Bite the tips of the front teeth together. Touch the tongue to the upper palate and focus the eyes on the tip of the nose. Place your hands comfortably on your lap. Mentally chant, "SA, TA, NA, MA" (Infinity, Life, Death, Rebirth) on the exhale breath for 15 minutes.

Health benefits

This tune-up affects the subconscious and offers great insights into the future. Mastery of this practice will heal the eyes.

Reflect once again about energy hygiene. Notice if any other personal beliefs have surfaced.

_____

_____

_____

_____

TEA PARTY VI

Teatime Tip: *Embracing an afternoon tea provides a soothing pause in a hectic world.*

Sample Menu

Dairy-Free Chocolate Avocado Mousse
Topped with Fresh Raspberries

Field Fresh Chamomile Tea

Conscious Contemplation
Chakras & Intuition

Teatime Tune-Ups
Healing the Heart Center
Enhance your Feeling

Recipe

Chocolate Avocado Mousse

Ingredients

½ cup raw cocoa powder
4-5 ripe avocados
½ cup maple syrup
3 teaspoons vanilla

1 teaspoon balsamic vinegar
1 teaspoon soy sauce
2 tablespoons coconut oil
Optional: 2 drops orange or peppermint essential oil
Fresh organic raspberries

Preparation

In a blender or food processor, combine avocados, cocoa powder, maple syrup, vanilla, vinegar, soy sauce, oil and blend well. Chill and serve in a fussy glass goblet. Garnish with raspberries and a large sprig of lemon leaf. For special occasions, add a chunk of chocolate to the garnish.

Tea

Chamomile

Known as a cure-all tea in most traditional folk medicine, German chamomile resembles daisy flowers and comes from the Matricaria recutita plant. With a calming sweetness, chamomile soothes the stomach and helps keep the blood alkaline. It has a strong anti-inflammatory and antifungal effect on the body. Enjoy a cup of chamomile before bed, and sleep like a baby.

Optional essential oil: add a drop of Rosemary and Slique oils to this infusion. Rosemary is known to stimulate memory and open the conscious mind. It's also great for viruses and wounds. Slique is a specialty-blended oil from Young Living that is used to maintain weight.

Conscious Contemplation

Chakras

The more we acknowledge our chakras (psychic centers) and become familiar with this system, the easier it is to incorporate them into our daily lives. When you come to a tea party, expect to examine your chakras.

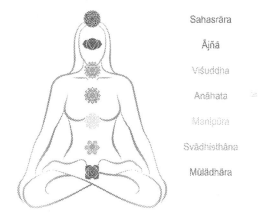

Sahasrära

Äjñä

Viśuddha

Anähata

Manipüra

Svädhisthäna

Mülädhära

As we learned in the *Conscious Dinner Parties* book, each dinner represented a specific chakra. These parties taught us the importance of knowing our dominant chakra energy. By knowing this information, we have insights into our true nature, personalities, life-purpose and health issues. Using this system can improve the daily quality of our lives.

Close your eyes, breathe then move into stillness. Slowly begin to feel areas in your body. Maybe your stomach hurts or your feet ache. Your throat or neck may feel heavy or uncomfortable. In Conscious Afternoon Teas, the body is the teacher, allowing the chakras to share their stories. The body communicates by using pain. Become aware of the tension that exists in your body and the related chakra energy that is being accessed. This is a powerful guide for self-healing. The body naturally shows us how to heal. All we need to do is close our eyes and step inward, find stillness and ask our bodies how we can support a healing journey. Then listen and feel. Learn to turn up the trust dial because an answer will soon appear.

The majority of us on this planet have been blessed with healthy bodies, so it is our duty to honor and care for them. Spiritual women who spend a lot of time in the higher chakras need to remember they are here for a human experience. It is time to get off the meditation cushion and go for a run in the park. The opposite is also true. People who are too earth-bound may need to put down the hamburger to pray and meditate. It is time to create a higher vibration and deeper spiritual connection. Learn to expand out from the 1st, 2nd and 3rd chakras. In other words, the body seeks equilibrium. Illness is simply the body's way of telling us that balance needs to be restored.

Maybe during a tea party, you feel pain in your chest. The heart chakra now is asking for attention. If the back of the chest hurts, there is a good chance you have unresolved issues of love or grief from your past. If the tension is in the front, this may be telling you that there is a problem with present day love and relationships. Regardless, it is time to pay attention.

Whatever chakra is asking for care, it is important to close your eyes, step within to find stillness and ask for some mental clarity. This is especially important if it is a dominant chakra that governs your entire health and well-being. In the end, tea parties help you develop a solid relationship with all your chakras.

Intuition

All of us have intuitive gifts to offer the world. Unfortunately, we don't always trust our gifts or rely on them for guidance. This can be a big mistake. Our spiritual greatness comes with our ability to tap into the angelic realm, God or source energy and our intuitive nature. These are resources for getting through life each day. Using our intuition can make a huge difference and can determine whether you thrive in life or just survive.

Close your eyes and move inward to find stillness. Seek out an area in the body that often gets your attention. We are looking for the dominant chakra, and if you can remember it from *Conscious Dinner Parties,* then immediately put your focus on that area. If you can't remember, then think about the area in your body that causes you the most pain and request most of your attention. Dominant chakras assist us as we discover an intuitive gift. There are four main intuitive forces linked to each of the seven major chakras. These intuitive gifts are the following: Clairvoyance, Claircognizance, Clairaudience and Clairsentience. Once you identify your dominant chakra, it will be fun to see what intuitive gift you have to offer the world.

Some women have the gift of Clairvoyance or clear seeing. You might be one of these women who can see spirits or senses the future. Maybe you are able to see a set of imagines being played out in the mind and minutes later this scenario gets played out again, only this time in real life. You might be a person who can immediately sense where a friend has lost her keys because you can actually see it in your mind's eye.

Claircognizance is clear knowing or having a gut feeling without any evidence to support your claims. Most women will have a gut feeling. How many times have you discounted any hunches and wished you hadn't? In time, honoring this inner-guidance and trusting what you know to be true will become a priority.

Many of you can hear spirit guides, weird voices, buzzing or pick up angelic music. If so, you have the gift of Clairaudience. Everyone has self-talk, but Clairaudience types are able to pick up unexplainable sounds that others can't hear. Usually one ear is set up to hear the messages. Women who are able to channel the spirit world are Mediums, known for their strong Clairaudience gift.

Clairsentience is clear feeling or being empathetic. Also, Clairsentience can be powerfully affected by touch, receiving messages from objects or personal belongings. Often Clairsentience can be the hardest gift to allow into your life and extremely difficult to manage if not grounded safely in the body.

All of us have an intuitive ability linked to our dominant chakra. Often there is more than one psychic gift available. This doesn't mean that tomorrow you will run out and become a psychic. It does mean that your life could become a little more mystical and spiritual if you pay attention to your chakras and intuitive gifts. The following is a list of the seven main chakras linked with one of the intuitive gifts discussed above:

Chakra Reference Guide

1st Chakra, Muladhara, *Clairsentience* or clear feeling is the intuitive gift of this chakra. The first chakra governs survival instincts, financial issues, self-image, family issues and the ability to function on the earth plane. The root chakra is located in the base of your spine.

2nd Chakra, Svadhishthana, *Clairvoyance* or clear seeing is the intuitive gift for this chakra. The second chakra is associated with creativity, birth, passion and manifesting ones purpose in a creative way. It is located below the navel in the womb area.

3rd Chakra, Manipura, *Claircognizance* or clear knowing is the intuitive gift of this chakra. The third chakra is our gut feeling. Personal power and self-esteem are important attributes of this area of the body. This chakra is located in the solar plexus and navel.

4th Chakra, Anahata, *Clairsentience* or clear feeling is the intuitive gift of this chakra. The fourth chakra is located in the chest. It is our heart energy and where we feel emotions. We use our heart chakra to forgive and show compassion toward others and ourselves. People with dominant heart energies are able to connect with many different types of people in order to be of service. It is considered a real honor to have dominant heart energy in a lifetime.

5ᵗʰ Chakra, Vishudda, *Clairaudience* or clear hearing is the intuitive gift of this chakra. The fifth chakra controls communication and is found at our throat and jaw area. This chakra acts as a portal that serves as a way for the spirit world to channel information that needs to be communicated back to the earth plane.

6ᵗʰ Chakra, Ajan, *Clairvoyance* or clear seeing is the intuitive gift for this chakra and is associated with the area in the middle of our forehead, referred to as "the third eye." Life is understood at a much deeper level. When this energy is dominant, it can bring forth ideas that have never been actualized on the earth plane. Women who have a strong dominant sixth chakra are known for being prophet-like.

7ᵗʰ Chakra, Sahasrara, *Claircognizance* or clear knowing is the power of the crown chakra. This is the area at the crown of your head and is associated with wisdom, the intellect, spiritual connection and divine inspiration.

What personal beliefs do you have about your intuition? Are you afraid to use this gift?

_____

_____

_____

_____

What personal beliefs do you have about chakras?

_____

_____

_____

_____

Is it easy for you to access your chakras?

_____

_____

_____

_____

Teatime Tune-Ups

Get Still––Inquire Actively––Live Consciously

Sit cross-legged, close your eyes and begin to connect with your sacred breath (5 minutes). Place your hands at your heart with fingertips and thumbs touching. The palms are apart so your hands create a ball in front of your heart. Close your eyes and begin inhaling 5 counts in, hold for 5 counts and exhale for 5 counts. Continue for 10 minutes. When finished, meditate on the heart.

Health benefits

This meditation helps to heal and open the heart. Along the way in life, our hearts can get quite a beating, so it is good to have a peaceful moment to connect with the heart energy and all its beauty. Emotional traumas end up being felt in the chest area. You might take your fingers and feel around for any sensitivity.

This tune-up can shift the heart energy and aid with healing breast cancer and lung problems. This tune-up also helps to clear the old emotions from the past, so you will feel more freedom in moving your shoulders and arms.

Reflect once again on the conscious contemplation of intuition and chakras. Notice if any other personal beliefs or prejudices have now surfaced.

TEA PARTY VII

Teatime Tip: *Drink your tea slowly, savoring its flavor and aroma. Fill the mind with pleasant peaceful thoughts.*

Sample Menu

Chilled Vegan Surprise Pumpkin Pie
Topped with a Sliver of Your Favorite Vegan Ice Cream

Lung Ching
An Earthy Chinese Green Tea
&
Chrysanthemum Tea

Conscious Contemplation
Essential Oils —Ancient Medicine

Teatime Tune-Ups
Relax and Renew to Maintain
A Healthy Aura

Recipe

Vegan Pumpkin Pie

Ingredients

Crust
1 cup sprouted almonds, ground
½ cup sprouted hazelnut, ground
½ cup sprouted walnuts, ground
10 soft-pitted dates, chopped
2 drops cinnamon essential oil

Filling

1½ cups coconut milk
1½ cups pumpkin puree from a medium fresh pumpkin
½ cup agave syrup
Pinch sea salt
1 teaspoon vanilla
2 drops cinnamon essential oil
2 drops ginger essential oil
2 drops clove essential oil
¼ teaspoon cardamom
4 teaspoons agar powder

Preparation

Two days before serving this dessert, sprout and dehydrate almonds and walnuts (not necessary for hazelnuts). In a large glass canning jar measure out the nuts and cover with purified water. Let the nuts sit overnight. The next day, place them in a dehydrator or oven at 150 degrees and allow them to dry. Then grind.

Preheat oven to 350 degree Fahrenheit.

In a large baking pan, place pieces of fresh pumpkin with rind side up. Fill the pan with a small amount of water (just enough to cover the bottom of the pan). Make sure to clear the seeds from the slices. Place pumpkin in oven and bake for 30-40 minutes.

In a large mixing bowl, combine the nuts (ground), dates and essential oil. Place the mixture into a deep round ceramic baking dish (no grease) and using the palm of your hands, firming press into a crust. Set aside.

Take baked pumpkin out of the oven, let cool. When the pumpkin can be easily handled, scoop into a mixing bowl and discard the outer skins. Puree with food processor.

In a large saucepan combine the pumpkin puree with the rest of the ingredients, except the agar. Bring to a simmer, then whisk in the agar for a couple of minutes. The agar will thicken the mixture. Remove filling from the heat, pour it into the crust and immediately refrigerate. Serve chilled with vegan ice cream.

Tea

Lung Ching

The Lung Ching tea is grown in Zehjiang, a Province of China. It has a fresh aroma with a jade-green color and is probably one of the most recognized green teas in the world. Its slightly sweet taste makes for a delightful afternoon tea. The leaves are dried and pressed in a hot wok then turned repeatedly until they obtain a flat shape.

In traditional Chinese medicine, practitioners have used green tea as a stimulant, diuretic, digestion aid and astringent. Studies show that green tea has the ability to regulate blood glucose density and lower the risk of heart disease.

Optional essential oil: add a couple drops of jasmine to this infusion. You might also want to place a couple more drops behind the ears. This oil helps alleviate depression with its uplifting aroma and will help create inner peace.

Conscious Contemplation

Essential oils are Ancient Medicines

The more spiritual a woman becomes, the more sensitive she is to the outside world. Certain foods, pollutants and medicines can easily upset this delicate gal.

For years, I struggled with the drugs prescribed by my doctors. I dealt with nasty skin rashes, nausea and other debilitating side affects.

About 20 years ago, my life shifted in an amazing way. I discovered essential oils and found my new supporting health tool. The oils would become a new medicine for my extra sensitive body. Now I cook, clean, take internally and apply pure, therapeutic, high-grade essential oils directly to the body when I need to feel supported.

It took a little time and discipline to study each oil's healing properties. As a result, grabbing the right oil for support these days has become effortless. Below I share one of my most recent essential oil success stories. Please enjoy.

A couple of years ago, I hosted a spiritual pilgrimage to Kerala, India. After the retreat, I notice a sore on my leg. Once back in Europe, this minor cyst started to get bigger, and within a month a golf-ball sized tumor had formed on my leg. I saw three Allopathic doctors and they all concurred, it had to come off immediately.

Surgery was sad news. As a medical intuitive, I know that cutting our bodies means interrupting the energy flow. Well, sometimes situations come into our life for a reason, so instead of resisting, I went under the knife. As I write, I realize that maybe this experience showed me at a very deep level the power of essential oils, so that years later, I could share this lesson.

The plastic surgeon removed the tumor. The cut was so deep you could see my shinbone. When it came time to heal, the surgeon suggested plastic surgery, which I immediately rejected. I told him I would heal myself. Soon, I felt very scared to be left alone with this major undertaking. How would I manage? This, my friend, is exactly the reason we don't get more personally involved in our own self-healing.

But as magic happens when you are a member of the supernatural highway club, the universe came to save the day once again. Out of the blue, an Ayurvedic doctor just happened to be traveling through Belgium on her way back to India and could help me start the healing process. *Praise the Lord.*

First, we used the leaves of a wild herb called comfrey. This herb was found growing along the side of the road in areas of Brussels. We cooked the roots and leaves down into a soupy consistency and when it was cooled, placed it directly on top of the wound. At the time, I was extremely overwhelmed, but soon learned to trust the Ayurveda doctor. She assured me this herb was being used in India for healing wounds like mine.

After several treatments of the comfrey, the doctor showed me how to apply Manuka honey from New Zealand to control infection along with several Young Living (pure, therapeutic-grade) essential oils for regenerating skin growth. The oils I chose were Melrose, Geranium and Helichrysum.

My leg healed beautifully. I never really shared this unorthodox healing method with my Italian plastic surgeon. His English wasn't the greatest and I just didn't know how supportive he would have been if he knew I was putting roadside herbs, honey and essential oils on a deep open wound. Since his training was in plastic surgery and not natural healing, I wasn't sure he would appreciation my self-healing technique.

I do believe the surgeon knew I was up to something. I had weekly visits with him to have the bandage changed and the wound examined. He told my husband in French that I must have a very healthy diet because my leg was healing extremely well. Hubby and I shared a glance and silently giggled.

There are so many successful healing stories when it comes to using essential oils. I have seen some extraordinary ways oils have helped people feel better, and in some cases completely restore their bodies back to a healthy state. For example, many women today suffer from severe depression. The following oils help release endorphins, keeping the blues away: Bergamot, Geranium, Myrrh, Rosewood, Ylang Ylang, Spruce, Hyssop, Mellissa, Rose, Tangerine, Jasmine and Lavender.

In serious cases, I have used oils internally in capsule form, as well as topically applying them directly to the pain. Essential oils have entered my kitchen and have taken my cooking to a whole new level. Burns from hot pans coming out of the oven are no longer a threat, as long as a bottle of Lavender oil is near. I have learned, in over 20 years of using essential oils, to always have them nearby to lighten the day and support my health.

Why Use Essential oils:
Supports modern health treatments
Supports multiple systems in our body
Treats almost all medical conditions
Better results from essential oil than from
prescription drugs

Young Living

It is stimulating to learn how these oils are distilled, what their healing properties are and ways to combine them with other oils for a successful outcome. Remember essential oils are very different from vegetable oils. These oils come straight from plants and are pure and high-grade. Essential oils and human blood share several common properties. Both contain hormone-like compounds, fight infections and initiate cell regeneration. The chemical structures of human cells and tissues are similar to the chemical structure of essential oils. This is what makes the oils compatible, readily identified and accepted by our bodies.

There are many different approaches to using essential oils. Since I have been out of the United States and living in Europe, I have read, and personally experienced, that the English are known for diluting essential oil with a small amount of vegetable oil and massaging them deep into the body. The French tend to use the oils as medicine and place them directly on the skin to be absorbed. The Germans have a totally different approach, as they focus on inhaling the oils. Essential oils, when inhaled, will stimulate the hypothalamus (the hormone command center of the brain) and limbic system (the seat of emotions). Research has shown this method to be effective in balancing the entire body.

No matter how you decide to use essential oils, they will serve your health. As I travel around the globe, I can immediately identify a person who uses essential oils just by their healthy glow and their higher vibration.

Below are a few examples of my personal successes with essential oils. My clients have shown me the power of dripping oils on the spine for deeper penetration. After a holistic essential oil session, they float out of my office. Remember, we are all different, so the way you use the oils will also be different. Try to muscle test on what application best supports your body. When using on a child, make sure to first dilute and test on a small area of the body for a reaction before applying. Always use caution when pregnant.

Here are a few essential oils and possible uses:
Young Living oils (YL) www.youngliving.org

- Geranium and Clary Sage placed directly below the navel and around the ankles to balance hormones
- Thieves (YL blend) on the bottom of the feet when you or your children feel symptoms of the flu
- Melaleuca clears up nail fungus
- Joy (YL blend) on the chest to heal issues of the heart and as a signature perfume
- Rose, Lavender and purified water as a mist for Rosacea (skin disorder)
- Rose for herpes
- Sage in water to create a mist to clear the energy in a room instead of a smoking sage stick
- PanAway (YL blend) for any muscle pain

- Orange combined with facial cleanser, skin lotions or in drinking water for extra antioxidants
- Endoflex (YL blend) around the neck to support the throat and thyroid gland
- Patchoull for winkles
- Di-Gize (YL blend) directly on the tummy for indigestion
- Lemon for baking, cleaning and in water for weight loss
- Grapefruit in drinking water for weight loss
- Balsam Fir and Peace & Calm (YL blend) used in a diffuser to create a peaceful home
- Clove for toothaches
- Vetiver for Attention Deficit Hyperactivity Disorder (ADHD)
- Nutmeg helps support the adrenal glands
- Oregano supports the body to rid parasites—it is a natural antibiotic
- Frankincense on the top of the head to remove negative energy and pain
- Marjoram for stiff joint pain
- Juniper supports the kidneys
- Jasmine uplifts the emotions
- Highest Potential (YL blend), Helichrysum and Frankincense reduce snoring
- Helichrysum reduces scarring and regenerates tissue growth
- Ginger prevents contagious diseases
- Eucalyptus is used for chest colds and flu
- Chamomile calms allergies
- White Angelica placed on the shoulders provides psychic protection
- Bergamot and Juvaflex (YL blend) support recovering from an addiction
- Bergamot and Geranium for Autism
- Raven (YL blend) supports the lungs; place on chest for coughs.

- Trauma Life (YL blend) for areas of the body that have sustained trauma
- Trauma Life (YL blend), Stress Away (YL blend) and Release (YL blend) support calming for Post Traumatic Stress disorder (PTSD)
- Dorado Azul is used for hormone balance
- RC (YL blend) for heal spurs
- GLF (YL blend) supports the liver and gallbladder
- Envision (YL blend) inhaled and placed on temples helps to manifest dreams
- Slique (YL blend) in water aids weight management
- Basel for calming muscle spasms

Chakras and essential oils

Below is a list of the main seven chakras in our bodies, which were discussed in the last party. To each chakra, I have added essential oils that can be used to support a healthy balance. If you are new to using essential oils, the list should help you get started. Smell the oils before applying them. If you find one repulsive, this oil is not for you. Don't use it. Take a couple drops of oil and place it directly on the body or along the spine and watch for magic to happen.

Chakra Reference Guide

1st **Chakra Muladhara** *Essential oils* to support the first chakra, skin and adrenal glands are: Grounding (YL blend), Valor, Vetiver, PanAway (YL blend), Inner-Child (YL blend), Cedarwood, Clove, Melrose, Melaleuca Alternifolia, Grapefruit, Copaiba, Cypress and Hinoki. Use the oil on the bottom of the feet, legs or tailbone.

2nd Chakra Svadhisthana *Essential oils* to support the second chakra and the reproduction glands are: Sandalwood, Ylang Ylang, Clary Sage, Fennel, Geranium, Dragon Time (YL blend), Melissa and Juniper. Place the oils directly on the pelvis or around the ankles.

3rd Chakra Manipura *Essential oils* to support the third chakra, the pancreas, liver, stomach and gallbladder are: Bergamot, Release (YL blend), Oregano, Aroma Siez (YL blend), JuvaFlex (YL blend), GLF (YL blend), Lime and Ginger. Place directly on the upper torso or on the bottom of the feet.

4th Chakra Anahata *Essential oils* to support the fourth chakra and the thymus gland are: Rose, Raven (YL blend), RC (YL blend), Marjoram, Yarrow, White Angelica and Joy (YL blend). Place directly on the chest.

5th Chakra Vishudda *Essential oils* to support the fifth chakra and the thyroid gland are: Eucalyptus, Sage, Frankincense, Exodus II, Myrrh, EndoFlex (YL blend) and Ocotea. Place the oils directly to the neck area with caution. If you are sensitive, dilute the oils.

6th Chakra Ajna *Essential oils* to support the sixth chakra and the pituitary gland are: Jasmine, Peppermint, Spearmint, Peace & Calming (YL blend), Charity (YL blend) and Lemongrass. Place a couple drops in your hands, and rub together then inhale.

7th Chakra Sahasrara *Essential oils* to support the seventh chakra and the pineal gland are: Helichrysum, Rose, Spruce, Frankincense, Palo Santo, Transformation (YL blend) and Basil. Inhale or apply directly on painful areas.

What personal beliefs do you have about using essential oils to support your body?

_____

_____

_____

_____

Close you eyes and breathe. What areas of your body need to be supported by an essential oil?

_____

_____

_____

_____

What oils do you currently use and what oils would you like to try?

_____

_____

_____

_____

Teatime Tune-Ups

Get Still––Inquire Actively––Live Consciously

Sit cross-legged, close your eyes and begin to connect with your sacred breath. After about 5 minutes, make cups with your hands with the palms facing up. The sides of the hands and pinkie fingers should be touching. Place your hands in front of your heart. Elbows are bent and your upper arms press against the ribs. Ask God for a blessing. Meditate on the Divine flow and feel the spirit move you. Stay in this position as long as you like.

Health benefits

This is a very restful meditation. The subtle pressure against the meridian points on the rib cage provides immediate relaxation to the body, mind and soul. Enjoy being showered by blessings, good health, abundance and happiness. Trust the universe to deliver a much deserved joyful feeling.

Reflect once again upon using therapeutic-grade essential oils as medicine. Notice if any other personal beliefs, fears or prejudices have now surfaced.

_____

_____

_____

_____

TEA PARTY VIII

Teatime Tip: *Remember to thank your friends for taking part in your nourishing tea ritual.*

Sample Menu

Orange Chocolate Molten Lava Cakes
Served with just a smidgen of vanilla ice cream

Lavender Blossom Tea

Conscious Contemplation
Archetypes

Teatime Tune-Ups
Balance Blood Pressure
Moon and Sun

Recipe

Orange Chocolate Molten Lava Cakes

Ingredients

1½ cups powdered honey
½ cup spelt flour
3 large eggs
3 egg yolks
1 cup raw cocoa powder

2/3 cup ghee
1 tablespoon vanilla
2 drops orange essential oil

Preparation

Preheat oven to 425 degree Fahrenheit.

Grease six (6-ounce) ramekins. Whisk eggs, yolks honey and ghee together then add cocoa, flour, vanilla and orange oil and continue to mix well. Fill ramekins with the cake batter and bake for 14 minutes. Serve hot with ice cream.

Tea

Lavender

Lavender is a very aromatic and slightly sweet tea. Lavandula angustifolia is the name of the lavender shrub. Use dried or fresh blossoms to create a beautiful pot of tea and, if you have extra, garnish the dessert plates with the beautiful violet buds. Serve this tea hot or cold and combine it with other favorite teas. Lavender goes especially well with chocolate.

This tea can help relieve the following: fatigue, inflammation, depression, digestion problems, nervousness and tension headaches. It is guaranteed to calm any and all stress.

Optional essential oil: add a couple drops of Fennel to this infusion. This oil is known to support hormonal balance.

Conscious Contemplation

Archetypes

Archetypes are connections to the collective unconscious and just possibly to our earliest ancestral families. As you step into deep stillness, you may find yourself drawn strongly toward a particular archetype. Your inner experience projects outward for all to see as you consciously bring forth a contracted persona. When we combine archetypes with intuition and chakras, there is a deep link to our psyche. Knowing this information about ourselves can add a little spice to an ordinary day. These patterns and behaviors can enhance everyone's life.

There are many ways to discover archetypal information, with all kinds of tests on the Internet. A psychic or astrologer can work with you. They may be able to create a report with a list of steps to follow as you embrace a certain archetype. However, the strongest path to finding a prominent archetype is to use your intuition and chakras to guide you on a mystic journey within.

In the personal story below, I had a little jump-start from another medical intuitive to help me recognize a dominant archetype of mine:

> I can't remember when it first started, but as long as I can remember I have had this obsession with wearing lipstick. I can't go out of the house until I have my lips painted. I blame my mother, as we all do for our funny quirks. I remember hearing her voice, "Honey, put your lipstick on, you will feel better."

I was worried my obsession was getting out of hand when one evening I experienced a bit of a panic as I quickly searched my purse for my lipstick. I was in the middle of a gathering of women, and we were scrambling to get ready to go into a sweat lodge. Most of the women were busy taking clothes off and preparing for the excess heat, but not me. I was too concerned with finding my lipstick. When the other women caught on to my dilemma, they teased me for the rest of the night.

I remembered the lipstick story from above when I recently traveled to Basal, Switzerland to attend a workshop given by one of my favorite teachers of all times, Caroline Myss. Before traveling to the event, I was thinking about Caroline's work around archetypes, so I fired off an email to one of her students who does psychic readings linking archetypes and astrology. I had been curious about this method so I gave her my birth chart and soon I received her feedback.

In my reading, the first house in my astrological chart had the Goddess Archetype. The report read, "You one of those women who can't leave the house without looking fabulous and of course you will always need your lipstick on to feel completely comfortable."

Now if someone ever comments or gives me a funny glance while I am refreshing my lips, I will hold my head up high and say, "Excuse me, I am a Goddess." I no longer worry about my lipstick obsession, and it feels good to be empowered.

Sometimes we go through life wondering why we are a certain way, and now there are tools to eliminate the guesswork. People poke fun at us all the time for our unique qualities and quirks. We often get embarrassed and lose our confidence. When we know who we are, then we can truly shine no matter what is being said about us.

Chakras

I discussed the chakra system in the two previous tea parties. Let's go into a little more detail by linking the archetypes with chakra energies. With the help of this system, you can start to design a personal profile listing all of your unique characteristics.

For instance, you have intense energy in the chest area. You notice people are drawn to you rather easily. It is as if you have been designed just to love everyone and always see only the goodness of a person. You have a big heart and people always comment on your loving nature. Now in your stillness, let your intuition guide you to experience a specific archetype in more detail. Discover ways to use this gift to be of greater service to mankind. Step into your heart chakra. Your archetype is that of the Caregiver, Lover, Goddess and Mother.

This is just one example and, as you move into stillness, you will discover much more. Use the chakras to guide you on this journey within. Start with the first, or base, chakra energy. Breathe deeply, close your eyes and find stillness. Ask yourself to identify strong archetypical energies. Listen and write down what has been conveyed. Proceed onto the second chakra until you have examined all seven of them. If you don't get clear answers right away, be patient.

You will discover contracted personas that you will not like. These are powerful archetypical energies that can impede and delay manifesting happiness. Make sure to note the ones that resonate with you. Allow yourself moments of stillness to ask about the following archetypes: Saboteur, Betrayer, Perfectionist, Victim, Villain, Temptress, Sycophant, Ordinary Man, Manipulator, Predator, Gossip, Hedonist, Loner, Slave and Martyr.

There are so many archetypes to examine. Spend some quality time and go within to discover them for yourself. Our tendency is to only want to know the powerful, attractive and beautiful sides of ourselves. No one wants to embrace the Saboteur. As you try to manifest opportunities and nothing is coming, you better believe the Saboteur is real in your persona and the sooner it is identified, the faster life will move forward. Open yourself up to the spirit world and ask for guidance on a deep subconscious level.

Exercise for Archetypes

Connect to stillness by slowly counting from 7 backwards: 7, 6, 5, 4, 3, 2, 1, 0. Now ask the spirit realm which of these personas exist within you during this lifetime. The following is a list of a few Archetypes: Hero, Innocent, Orphan, Survivor, Athlete, Rebel, the Healer, Visionary, Explorer, Creator, Alchemist, Artist, the Leader, Guardian, Ruler, the Mother, Caretaker, Lover, Performer, Intellectual, Advocate, Royal, Channel, Explorer, Teacher, Prophet, Dreamer, Magician, The Spiritual Master, Scholar, Sage, Saboteur, Betrayer, Perfectionist, Victim, Villain, Temptress, Sycophant, Ordinary Man, Manipulator, Predator, Gossip, Hedonist, Loner, Slave and Martyr.

Chakra Reference Guide

Below you will find the qualities associated with each chakra in previous tea parties compiled in one list. Archetypes have been added. Hopefully, you will start to appreciate the valuable role chakras play in our daily lives. Refer often to the list below:

1ˢᵗ **Chakra, Muladhara,** The *Archetypes* are: Hero, Innocent, Orphan, Survivor and Rebel. This chakra is known for the intuitive gift of Clairsentience and governs survival instincts, financial issues, self-image and the ability to function on the earth plane. The root chakra is located in the base of your spine. Essential oils to support the first chakra, skin and adrenal glands are: Grounding (YL blend), Valor, Vetiver, PanAway (YL blend), Inner-Child (YL blend), Cedarwood, Clove, Melrose, Melaleuca Alternifolia, Grapefruit, Copaiba, Cypress and Hinoki.

2nd **Chakra, Svadhishthana,** The *Archetypes* are: Healer, Creator, Alchemist and Artist. This chakra is known for the intuitive gift of Clairvoyance and is associated with creativity, birth and passion. The second chakra is located below the navel in the womb area. Essential oils to support this chakra and the reproduction glands are: Sandalwood, Ylang Ylang, Clary Sage, Fennel, Geranium, Dragon Time (YL blend), Melissa and Juniper.

3rd **Chakra, Manipura,** The *Archetypes* are: Leader, Guardian and Ruler. This chakra has the intuitive gift of Claircognizance. The third chakra is connected to our gut feelings and knowing who can be trusted. Personal power and self-esteem are important attributes. This chakra is located in the solar plexus and navel. Essential oils to support the third chakra, the pancreas, liver, stomach and gallbladder are: Bergamot, Release (YL blend), Raven (YL blend), RC (YL blend), Oregano, Aroma Siez (YL blend), JuvaFlex (YL blend), GLF (YL blend), Lime and Ginger.

4th **Chakra, Anahata,** The *Archetypes* are: Mother, Caretaker, Lover and Goddess This is our heart energy and where we feel emotions. It is known for having the intuitive gift of Clairsentience. We use our heart chakra to forgive and show compassion toward others and ourselves. We are able to connect with many different types of people in order to be of service. It can be considered a real honor to have dominant heart energy. Essential oils to support the fourth chakra and the thymus gland are: Rose, Marjoram, Yarrow, White Angelica and Joy (YL blend).

5ᵗʰ Chakra, Vishudda, The *Archetypes* are: Medium, Explorer and Teacher. Clairaudience is the intuitive gift of this chakra and it controls communication. The fifth chakra is located in the neck area. The throat acts as a portal that serves as a way for the spirit world to channel information that needs to be communicated back to the earth plane. Essential oils to support the fifth chakra and the thyroid gland are: Eucalyptus, Sage, Frankincense, Exodus II, Myrrh, EndoFlex (YL blend) and Ocotea.

6ᵗʰ Chakra Ajna The *Archetypes* are: Prophet, Dreamer and Magician. This chakra is associated with the intuitive gift of Clairvoyance, or clear seeing, and it governs intuition. The sixth chakra is located in the middle of our forehead and is referred to as "the third eye." This chakra helps us understand life at a much deeper level. When it is activated, ideas will appear that have never been actualized on the earth plane. Women who have a strong dominant sixth chakra are known to be prophet-like. Essential oils to support the sixth chakra and the pituitary gland are: Jasmine, Peppermint, Spearmint, Peace & Calming (YL blend), Charity (YL blend) and Lemongrass.

7ᵗʰ Chakra Sahasrara The *Archetypes* are: Spiritual Master, Scholar and Sage. Claircognizance is the intuitive gift of the crown chakra. The seventh chakra is located at the crown of the head and is associated with wisdom, the intellect, spiritual connection and divine inspiration. Essential oils to support this chakra and the pineal gland are: Helichrysum, Rose, Spruce, Frankincense, Palo Santo, Transformation (YL blend) and Basil.

Notice the Archetypes that appeal to you and add them to your list:

_____

_____

_____

_____

Can you see how these Archetypes could be helpful with your life's journey? Describe.

_____

_____

_____

_____

What personal beliefs do you have about Archetypes?

_____

_____

_____

_____

Teatime Tune-Ups

Get Still––Inquire Actively––Live Consciously

Sit cross-legged, close your eyes and begin to connect with your sacred breath (5 minutes). Stretch your legs out and come back to a cross-legged position. Make sure your spine is straight as you do this exercise.

For **high blood pressure**, take your right thumb and close off your right nostril. The fingers of your right hands are straight up in the air. Begin deep breathing or Breath of Fire. This is breathing through your nose while the navel is being pumped. If you have ever watched a puppy pant, their stomach moves in and out quickly as they breathe. Now use that example and close your mouth and breathe through your nose. See if you can recreate the same panting action above the navel center (solar plexus area). If not, then just take long deep breaths. Continue for 3 minutes. For long-standing high blood pressure, carry out this breathing daily for 40 minutes without the Breath of Fire.

Low blood pressure uses the opposite movement. Take the left thumb and close the left nostril and begin with deep breathing or Breath of Fire for 3 minutes. The same holds true for long-standing problems with low blood pressure; carry out this exercise daily for 40 minutes without the Breath of Fire.

Health benefits

This healing ritual balances your blood pressure. If you are taking blood pressure medication, it is okay to do this tune-up. Over time, you will discover that you may not need medication any longer.

Reflect once again on Archetypes. Notice if any other new beliefs or resistances have surfaced.

_____

_____

_____

_____

TEA PARTY IX

Teatime Tip: *Invite A Divine source and your higher self to every afternoon tea.*

Sample Menu

Mini Blueberry Muffins

*India's Finest Traditional
Black Chai Tea
&
Rooibos Chai*

*Conscious Contemplation
Waking Up To A New World*

*Teatime Tune-Ups
The Quest for Wholeness*

Recipe

Mini Blueberry Muffins

Ingredients

1 cup spelt flour
½ cup almond flour
2 tablespoons chia seeds

2 teaspoons baking powder
Pinch salt sea
½ cup agave syrup
1/3 cup ghee
1 egg
1/3 cup milk
½ teaspoon vanilla
2 cups fresh organic blueberries

Preparation

Preheat oven to 400° Farenheit. Grease one, 12-cup mini muffin tin or use paper liners.

In a large mixing bowl, whisk agave and ghee together, then blend in milk and egg. Add flour, seeds, baking powder, vanilla and salt. Mix well. Gently fold in the blueberries. Fill to the top for a full muffin top. Bake for 8-10 minutes. This recipe yields 24 mini muffins.

Tea

Black Chai Tea

Chai tea from India is a spicy, pungent drink made from some of the most medicinally active herbs. The basic components of chai include black tea, cinnamon, ginger, clove, cardamom and black pepper. This tea is delicious served with warm milk and honey.

Chai tea has been used to support digestion, prevent cancer, lower blood sugar, promote cardiovascular health and serves as a powerful antioxidant.

Optional essential oil: add one drop of Bergamot to this infusion to help release stress.

Conscious Contemplation

Waking Up to a New World

When a major life crisis or health issue enters into our lives, this can be a sure sign of a spiritual emergency. As an energy healer, this is a prime theme I explore at Conscious Afternoon Teas. A spiritual emergency, also called a spiritual awakening or, as we have now discovered, a Kundalini Rising experience, is worth our time to examine more closely. A thought-provoking documentary film called *Spiritual Emergency* by Kajal Nightingales can explain this subject matter in greater detail. During the last tea party, set some extra time aside to watch this film and note any strong reactions.

Some interesting statistics stood out to me after watching this documentary. The film mentions that 50% of young kids, 14 years and under will have a spiritual awakening, with another 25% experiencing one at around 25 years of age. So 75% of young adults will awaken to a new world before their 30th birthday. To whom will they turn for help? As a global force, are we even paying attention to our young adults and their cries for assistance?

The BBC news presented more statistics in a recent evening broadcast. According to 2014 studies, more money is being spent on mental illness, and this has become a top concern for Great Britain and other countries around the world. The report mentioned that the problem begins with young kids around 14 years of age. The important questions being asked are how to address this issue and what is the major cause behind this growing number of mental illness cases.

Maybe it is time for some of these instances to be called by their rightful name, a spiritual awakening. It is important to consider that the mentally afflicted might just be people like you and me who are having a spiritual awakening. We really need to understand that young people today are having spiritual shifts with weak inner support systems and no teacher to guide them. Women, we can only do something about this significant issue if we become aware.

Ancient and preindustrial cultures placed a high value on spiritual awakenings and non-ordinary states of consciousness. Unfortunately, the advent of the industrial and scientific revolution dramatically changed the Western world and the way we perceive basic wellness. Many Folk religions around the world still embrace spiritual awakenings as a very normal rite of passage. These cultures have been handling these emergences with integrity and grace. For example, what Western psychiatry labels acute schizophrenia, a South African tribe would call a prerequisite for initiation into priesthood.

Folk religions can offer the Western world tips on how to create a safe space to transition and transform levels of consciousness. Instead of labeling their youth as mentally ill and feeding them full of anti-depressants or anti-psychotics, they usher their children into a new world with a spiritual vision quest. The child goes out into nature with a master teacher and comes back transformed into an adult. This has been a successful standard protocol for centuries.

These ancient religions acknowledge nature and the spirit realm as a way of life. Magic and mystical experiences are part of their culture. Sympathetic magic is a common force that influences other common forces in life, much like the collective unconscious. The following are some examples of folk practices that help create this magical force and influence shifts in consciousness:

- Chanting, fasting, sacred trance dance
- Deep breathing exercises
- Rituals to ward off evil spirits
- Fertility, birthing and dying rites
- Vision quests, studying dreams
- Hoodoo, Voodoo, Pow-Wow and Santeria
- Spiritual altars and shrines
- Reincarnation and past lives

- Veneration of saints
- Faith healing and folk medicine with herbs
- Burning incense or sage to create a sacred ritual
- The use of psychedelic drugs like DMT to create an altered state
- Taoist–Tai Chi
- Judaic–spinal rocking
- Yoga

In a time when we barely have a sacred moment for tea, entertaining a vision quest may not be a viable option. Where would you turn, then, if an awakening happened to you or to your daughter? Who could you talk to about this situation? We all have a list of doctors to call in case of an emergency, but this is a bit different. You might call a psychologist, which is fine, but maybe stop and reconsider for a moment. Are you really going mad or just experiencing a new world with some unexplainable spiritual twists?

I suggest first seeking out a person who has gone through an awakening to come to your aid. A *wake-up doula* would be the perfect person to have on hand. Find someone who can help birth your new spiritual persona and safely guide you through higher levels of consciousness.

In the past, if a person heard voices or had visions of a spiritual nature, they were often diagnosed as showing signs of a mental disorder. Talking out loud to spirit guides in some circles would be discouraged. However, there is good news to share. Recently in psychology, a new area of treatment has been created specifically for spiritual and religious problems. This is a positive step forward in healthcare and might just create a safer place to birth a spiritual awakening.

Attention: If your delusions are a danger to yourself or another, then immediately call for help or seek a professional. Use the references below. The goal of an awakening is to experience this transformation with gentle, loving grace. Suicide attempts or threats to others are not part of a gentle wake-up. This should not be taken lightly and requires our full attention.

Support Networks around the world:

Czech Republic www.diabasis.cz
Germany www.senev.de
UK www.SpiritualCrisisNetwork.org.uk
USA www.spiritualemergence.info/
Australia www.spiritualemergence.org.au
Canada www.spiritualemergence.net

I was in my late 20s when I met an unusual psychiatrist. He was my wake-up doula and he did not prescribe drug therapy or hospitalization. He must have been sent by angels to forewarn me of what was in store for my life as a spiritually and intuitively gifted woman. He told me the voices I heard, the visions I had and the spirits I could see were due to my deep connection to the spirit world. My spiritual awakening transition would be mild, and my purpose was to help other people with their spiritual journeys. The good doctor also mentioned specifically that I would teach women about chakras. Mostly he highlighted that I should be cautious when working with medical and mental health systems, because they would try to medicate me for my intuitive gifts. Years later, I have lived out all of his predictions.

My Aunt Helen, on the other hand, wasn't as lucky. According to my mother, my aunt was an empath who could feel other people's energy and heard voices. We shared similar gifts. She was diagnosed with Schizophrenia, institutionalized for months and given multiple electric shock treatments. When she returned home to the farm, she was not the same. The treatments caused a lot of damage to her brain.

Being intuitive is not an illness. It is a gift and should be treated as one. It is truly up to us how we handle our transformations. When you are going through a spiritual awakening, stay conscious. If you start to feel overwhelmed, immediately seek out your teacher, and back off from some of the daily practices that heighten your energy. It is time to find the earth and stay grounded. Also, alcohol and drugs are not your friends during an intense awakening.

If you are in this place right now on your journey, please reference the following books: *The Call of Spiritual Emergency* by Emma Bragdon, *In Case Of Spiritual Emergency* by Catherine Lucas or *Saints and Madmen* by Russell Shorto. These references and a good spiritual wake-up doula will be very helpful as you journey into deeper levels of consciousness.

If you have spent a lifetime without a defined spiritual practice, then of course you might be alarmed with your spiritual shifts. If you all of sudden hear voices from above or start seeing spirits, then it is a good sign an awakening is on its way. However, if you have kept a close connection with the spirit realm since birth, then a spiritual emergence can make a whole lot of sense, and it won't come as such a surprise.

We live in an age when we don't need to fear being burned at the stake for acknowledging our spiritual and intuitive gifts. We can safely awaken without fearing excessive drug treatments or being locked up in an institution. It is safe to be a bit different. Normal is way overrated. My personal advice is to do your Kundalini Yoga and have a wake-up doula available, just in case. What had been labeled dangerous, psychotic, altered states of consciousness are now being rejuvenated in the 21st century as beautiful spiritual awakenings and an invitation into a bright new world.

Jyl Auxter

Illness

Shamanism is humanity's most ancient religion and healing art. Many witch doctors or medicine men and women go through what anthropologists have labeled a Shamanic illness as their spiritual awakening. This is how a psycho-spiritual crisis turns into a blessing. The Shaman understands that this is part of the process and is the true initiation into becoming a master healer. The healer must first heal him or herself. An illness, in this case, is not considered a broken body, but rather a rite of passage to launch the soul to higher states of consciousness.

So why, then, is a heart attack not simply called a spiritual emergency or unbalanced energy of the heart? And why would we ever want to cut into our hearts? This is something I have never clearly understood as an energy healer. Why isn't a problem with the gallbladder thought of as an unresolved issue in the 3rd chakra? And why not examine a person's emotional issues around this dominant energy? Instead of treating a healing crisis as a mechanical problem of a broken down body, why not reconsider illnesses as a spiritual shift?

This is our new task-at-hand. We must learn to empower ourselves to self-heal, then start sharing these experiences with others. A major shift in medicine is coming. We are bringing back the ancient ways with a new vibration. Why not start today and prepare for this new change in self-healing.

About ten years ago, I was in La Jolla, California teaching a yoga class. After the practice was finished, two men approached me with questions. They wanted to know more about my work as a medical intuitive. They were especially interested in knowing more about energy medicine and how it worked. Both men were surgeons from Miami, Florida, and they were just in the city for a couple of days on vacation.

We talked for a while and one of the doctors told me that he was a retired heart surgeon. He had been spending much of his time reading and studying Integrated Medicine. He told me energy medicine had made him rethink heart surgery. After a long discussion, the heart surgeon walked out of the yoga studio with his friend uttering, "Knowing now what I know to be true about energy medicine, I would have never cut on a person's heart."

Our ailments are simply signs we need to restore our balance. It is most likely a healing opportunity that requires spiritual growth. At a soul level, an illness might actually be preparing you for a powerful change in your life. Viewing illness as the enemy is antagonistic and counterproductive. Instead, maybe it is time to look at disease as a partner that has come to help you learn more about your soul's journey here on earth. Expand your thinking around sickness. I realized this reasoning might go beyond your current beliefs, but lower any resistance and try to stay open.

Throughout my life, I've always looked at an ailment as an excuse for a little personal down time to recalibrate. Who knows, our souls might have agreed to a shift in consciousness by creating a complaint. Our higher self has arranged an awakening at a certain age in our life, and BAM, a sickness comes out of nowhere. Another possibility, that might be a bit *out-of-the-box* in your thinking, is that before reincarnating you might have agreed to clear soul contracts on behalf of your ancestral line. This is an honor and a powerful opportunity to do some important deep, karmic cleaning on behalf of previous generations. It is up to us to stay empowered when faced with an illness or major life change. Use this as opportunity to grow spiritually and unite with an unfathomable inner peace.

If you know anyone who has gone through a near death experience, usually they come back an exceptionally changed person. The same is true for someone who is involved in a debilitating illness, loses a limb or suffers from acute pain. Warriors coming back from fighting with post-traumatic stress disorder (PTSD) also need to readjust and recalibrate.

Filling people up with drugs retards their spiritual shifts in consciousness. I believe the soul, in conjunction with the spirit world, directs our journeys. A spiritual awakening is our teacher, and it can truly be a gift of a lifetime, depending on how you look at it. I like to think that everything in life is happening for a reason, and we are fully in charge. You don't need to agree right away with this approach, but promise me you will ruminate on this idea during tea.

Conscious Afternoon Teas can be a place to anchor crazy ideas. In time, you will see that your off-the-wall, crazy notions are not so outlandish. Other women will come to honor spiritual awakenings. Change is occurring, whether we like it or not. It is time to embrace a New World.

Everyone will experience a shift in consciousness. How will you embrace yours?

_____

_____

_____

_____

All of us have the right to a peaceful life. How will you receive yours?

_____

_____

_____

_____

Does this topic bring up fear? Describe.

_____

_____

_____

_____

Teatime Tune-Ups

Get Still—Inquire Actively —Live Consciously

Sit cross-legged, close your eyes and begin to connect with your sacred breath (5 minutes). Stretch out your legs and then come back to a cross-legged position. Sit up straight, and make a fist of your hands. Extend the thumbs out and place them on either side of your head at the temple area where you can feel a pulse. Press down on the back molars of your teeth and see if you can feel the pulse under your thumbs. The chant, "SA, TA, NA, MA" (Infinity, Life, Death, Rebirth) is done silently.

Begin by placing your thumbs to your temple and locking (pressing down) your back molars with a closed mouth. As you silently say, "SA"—press down, "TA"—press down, "NA"—press down, "MA"—press down. Continue on for 5 minutes. Create a rhythm with your breath and the firm pressure of your thumb.

Health benefits

This meditation is excellent for everyone. It is particularly effective for drug dependency, mental illnesses and phobic conditions. It also works on subconscious addictions that lead us to insecure or neurotic behavior patterns, like dependencies and feelings of unworthiness.

Reflect once again about the life lesson above. Notice if any other personal beliefs or prejudices have surfaced.

_____

_____

_____

_____

PART V

Conscious Living

A round the late 1800s, tea had become a widely accepted beverage in Europe. This was a time when most coffee and teahouses had evolved into clubs exclusively for men. Women were only allowed in teashops and tea gardens with a male escort. As a result, women started to invite friends and family into their homes to share a conversation over a fussy cup of afternoon tea. In today's high stress world, afternoon tea in your home is an opportunity for a retreat.

The time has come for all of us to create inner peace and find a moment to reflect upon our lives. Living a life with tension and stress might work for a while in our 20s, and even into our early 30s. However, moving into your 40s, 50s and 60s with a demanding lifestyle can catch up to you and start to cause major health concerns. It doesn't take long before an angry world starts to seep into our cells and take over. We all meet women who look calm and collected on the outside, but on the inside, watch out, because they are ready to blow. Unresolved emotional issues will take a toll on our health. It is our job as women to offer a helping hand to girlfriends who may be going through a crisis. This is the perfect time to invite them to Conscious Afternoon Teas. These events offer an invaluable healing experience.

Jyl's Conscious Afternoon Teas

I hold 21st century Conscious Afternoon Teas around the world with multicultural women from every walk of life. These women represent many different religious backgrounds. Any religious differences are seldom discussed. The afternoon teas provide a forum for acceptance and safety as women learn to explore metaphysics with curiosity.

The joy for me, personally, is to escort ladies to an empowered place within and watch them transform and heal with my own eyes. I am not there to show off some special intuitive gifts. These gatherings are about reminding other women of their own abilities and coaching them when necessary. Intuitive gifts, if not used, can be a human waste when there are so many sad and lonely souls out there who could use our help. In the past, some teas offered a healing circle, where the women were asked to connect deeply with their physical bodies. Other times, we examined chakras with a goal of understanding health and our greater purpose. Sometimes, we discussed what it meant to be intuitive and considered beneficial ways to use this powerful gift.

Often, gentle yoga was included during the tea parties to help the ladies detoxify and prepare their bodies for deeper spiritual experiences, linked to a higher physical vibration. Some teas turned into holistic cooking and nutrition classes. Many women seemed to have a strong need for healing support around diets.

Our discussions sometimes led to understanding efficient ways to use our energies. Teaching concepts like, "how to avoid leaking precious life force," has offered much insight to women, as they learn to maintain solid boundaries and good health.

Each tea has always been beautifully orchestrated and spiritually channeled to support the group and myself. All I had to do was show up as a conduit for the spirit world and let the magic in. The gals most committed to these gatherings are spiritual women who have had a religious or spiritual practice and want to go deeper into self-inquiry and self-discovery. These ladies are serious about their spiritual quest. They want to connect deeply with their inner mystic, and to them this was not a *woo-woo* connection. This was a serious life saving experience and a life altering transformation.

I wrote this book not to fill your mind full of complex facts and answers. On the contrary, I wrote it to stimulate questions and help you grow.

Brighter Days

Women have so much power in the area of spiritual inspiration. It might be hard to accept this opportunity as a chance to become a true influencer and to help the world advance. Some of us are still asleep and will consider examining our spiritual and religious nature to be an extreme burden. We may feel safer holding onto our suffering, rather than excited about seeing a change in the world. Other women may choose to stay unconscious by allowing old, outdated religious beliefs and prejudices to become distractions, clouding any deeper, spiritual truths.

It is time to wake up and march forward, to teach our children and grandchildren the ways of a spiritual being. It is time to own our power and educate the world about spiritual greatness. I would have to say, "It is time for a Conscious Afternoon Tea."

On the spiritual front, women are empowered to enjoy the Divine in a personal way, with less pressure to belong to a congregation. In the West, this freedom is our choice, and we can either accept it or not. We can easily accept all the knowledge brought forth from the past if it represents love. There's no need for a high-pressure sales job to promote religion or spirituality. The Source truly doesn't need to be sold if authentic, spiritual women come forth out of their closets and caves. We are long overdue for fresh, genuine teachers to share loving messages in the world. Check in with yourself to see if you are up for this duty.

Women will bring the ancient legends of the past into present day acceptance with a positive flair. It will be up to us to encourage a gentle flow of spiritual exchange in the world, while keeping ourselves balanced and healed. Women will nurture mystical emergence or non-ordinary states of consciousness as something that naturally happens when spiritual growth occurs. It is time to heal our families and lead them into a new world with our heads held high and teacups in hand.

Final words

My gratitude goes to all the women who read this book. I hope you have enjoyed the tea parties in all their glory. The value of this book lies in your level of commitment to the cause. Are you up to the task of trying a new recipe and tasting an unfamiliar tea? Will you allow yourself a sacred time-out to ponder, meditate and heal unresolved issues?

The teatime tune-ups are meant to help you feel a new vibration and with time, a trusted altered state of consciousness. Each of the tune-ups can be incorporated into your daily routine. The most precious and powerful gift you could give yourself is a timeout to develop inner peace.

I send love to all yogis, especially to my old yoga student who was mentioned earlier in the book. I hope she no longer restricts herself from a prayer of any type. It is time for all of us to encourage spiritual expansion instead of religious contraction. I see many changes in the Western world's future, with all of our religious freedoms and spiritual rights. When a ritual like yoga is done on a regular basis, expect a major transition. Yoga was intended to lead the yogi into personal greatness and a deep spiritual connection.

Please join me as I host a Conscious Afternoon Tea in a location near you. Learn what it means to be peaceful, healthy and a true mystic. Blessings, and see you soon.

Jyl

REFERENCES
BOOKS, ARTICLES & WEBSITES

"Consciousness" in the Stanford Encyclopedia of Philosophy

The Yoga of the Bhagavad Gita by Self-Realization Fellowship

Essays of World Religions by Houston Smith

Toward A Super-Consciousness, Meditational Theory & Practice by Hiroshi Motoyama

The Kundalini Yoga Experience by Guru Dharam Khalsa & Darryl O'Keeffe

Eight Limbs, The Yoga Suttras of Patanjali

Kundalini Rising by Gurmukh Kaur Khalsa, Sivananda Radha et al.

What's Cooking Within by www.jylauxter.com

Young Living Essential Oils www.youngliving.com

Teatime Tunes Ups Healing Ritual, Kundalini Kriyas by Yogi Bhajan

Spiritual Emergency, When Personal Transformation Becomes a Crisis by Stanislav Grof. M.D. and Christina Grof

Flours Reference, Diabetic Living Online

Tea Timeline Reference, Tea.co.uk

Major Religions of the World Ranked by number of Adherents, Adherents.com

Tea Reference, Teaviews.com

Saints and Madmen by Russell Shorto

Other books and products by the author:

Books

Conscious Dinner Parties…A Girlfriend's Guide to 9 Transformational Gatherings

What's Cooking Within?…Yoga, Meditation and Recipes

Yoga DVDs:

Healing Yoga

Dessert Gentle Yoga

For more information on Jyl's International Workshops & Retreats, Private Energy Healing Sessions and Conscious Parties, email jylauxter@aol.com or visit www.jylauxter.com.

Printed in the United States
By Bookmasters